Bloom's

GUIDES

Toni Morrison's
Beloved

1984
All the Pretty Horses
Beloved
Brave New World
Cry, The Beloved Country
Death of a Salesman
Hamlet
The Handmaid's Tale
The House on Mango Street
I Know Why the Caged Bird Sings
The Scarlet Letter
To Kill a Mockingbird

Bloom's
GUIDES

Toni Morrison's
Beloved

Edited & with an Introduction
by Harold Bloom

CHELSEA HOUSE
PUBLISHERS
A Haights Cross Communications ✔ Company
Philadelphia

© 2004 by Chelsea House Publishers, a subsidiary of Haights Cross Communications.

A Haights Cross Communications Company

Introduction © 2004 by Harold Bloom.

Printed and bound in the United States of America.

First Printing
1 3 5 7 9 8 6 4 2

Library of Congress Cataloging-in-Publication Data
Applied For
ISBN: 0-7910-7570-2

Chelsea House Publishers
1974 Sproul Road, Suite 400
Broomall, PA 19008-0914

www.chelseahouse.com

Contributing editor: Amy Sickels

Cover series and design by Takeshi Takahashi

Layout by EJB Publishing Services

Contents

Introduction

Harold Bloom

No dispute exists or ought to be fostered concerning Toni Morrison's strength as a literary artist. *Paradise* (1998) confirmed yet once more her eminence at story-telling and as a prose stylist. Morrison herself has implied that the proper context for reading and studying her must be found primarily in African-American women writers. On that view, Ralph Ellison is as unlikely a candidate for comparison as would be William Faulkner, Virginia Woolf, or Cormac McCarthy. And yet Toni Cade Bambara and Alice Walker do not help much in contextualizing Morrison. The most distinguished African-American novel by any woman save Morrison is certainly Zora Neale Hurston's *Their Eyes Were Watching God*, a book totally remote from Morrison's mode and vision. Toni Morrison, like Faulkner and Cormac McCarthy, is a high rhetorician. Like Virginia Woolf, Morrison is a mythological and historical fantasist. *Beloved* purports to be a true history of African-American slavery. The critic Stanley Crouch, disputing Morrison's version of history, rather unkindly termed *Beloved* a soap opera of the Black Holocaust. Few have agreed with Crouch; *Beloved* is central to the current canon of literature read and studied in American schools and colleges. I myself come neither to praise nor dispraise *Beloved*, but only to ask some questions about the book. Perhaps *Beloved* is a permanent work, perhaps not. In time, it may be regarded as a brilliant period piece, perfectly revelatory of the cultural age of Ideological Resentment, through which we continue to pass.

Beloved divides many of my acquaintances who possess critical discernment; for some of them it is a masterwork, for others it is supermarket literature. I myself am divided: no character in the novel persuades me, and yet much of this writing has authentic literary force. Few narratives since *Uncle Tom's Cabin* are as tendentious as *Beloved*; Morrison has a palpable design to impose upon her readers, and nothing in the book seems accidental or incidental. The novel is, to some extent, a punishment for black and white, male and female alike. The enormities of the horrors being represented give some authority to Morrison's moral judgments, implicit and explicit.

And yet there are virtually insurmountable aesthetic problems in the representation of any Holocaust, whether of six million Jews or of the "sixty million" African Americans to whom Morrison dedicates *Beloved*. Something in our psychic defenses is activated by a litany of atrocities that comprehends mammary rape, a mother's cutting of her baby's throat, whippings, dreadful prison treatment on chain gangs—I stop arbitrarily, rather than complete the catalog. However veiled by indirect style or supernatural intercessions, this profusion of torments may numb any reader's sensibilities. "Guilt is never to be doubted," the motto of Franz Kafka's penal colony, is not necessarily a formula for aesthetic achievement. Acknowledging culpability, at whatever level, itself can become an evasion of cognitive and aesthetic standards of judgment.

Since every critical view excerpted in this volume assumes the literary greatness of *Beloved*, I find myself the odd fellow out, but that may have some value for the student and the reader. In my own judgment, Morrison's authentic novels are *Sula* and *Song of Solomon*, the latter still her masterpiece. Morrison's prophetic and political vocation tends to make *Beloved* and *Jazz* somewhat problematic works for me. I conclude tentatively by noting again Morrison's remarkable ongoing gifts, that perhaps have found better balance between ideology and story-telling in *Paradise*.

Biographical Sketch

Toni Morrison, the second of four children, was born Chloe Anthony Wofford on February 18, 1931, to George and Ramah Willis Wofford in Lorain, Ohio. Her mother, a housewife, and her father, a shipyard welder, had both moved from the South to escape racism and to find better opportunities for themselves and their children. The Woffords taught their children to appreciate black literary culture by singing and reading African folklore to them at an early age; not surprisingly, Morrison was the only child in her first grade class who knew how to read upon entrance. Morrison was an avid reader and an enthusiastic literary student from the start. She took her education seriously and graduated with honors from Lorain High School in 1949.

Morrison entered the prestigious Howard University in Washington, D.C., in the fall of 1949, majoring in English with a minor in classics. She graduated from Howard University with a Bachelor of Arts degree in English in 1953. Morrison went on to continue her education at Cornell, writing her thesis on suicide in the works of William Faulkner and Virginia Woolf and receiving her M.A. in 1955. Morrison began teaching English at Texas Southern University in Houston later that year. In 1957, however, she decided to return to Washington, D.C. to accept an English faculty position at Howard University. Soon after, she met and fell in love with Harold Morrison, a Jamaican architect.

In 1958, she married Harold Morrison and they had two children, Harold Ford and Slade Kevin. Due mostly to cultural differences, the couple divorced in 1964. After taking a brief trip to Europe, Morrison moved back to her hometown and in with her parents in Lorain, Ohio.

Morrison stayed with her parents for less than a year, and in 1965 she moved to Syracuse, New York, to become a textbook editor for a subsidiary of Random House. Then, in 1967, she transferred to New York City and was promoted to senior editor; she specialized in black fiction, nurturing such talents as Angela Davis and Toni Cade Bambara. She also taught English part-time at two separate branches of the State University of New York. She remained at Random House until 1984, when she was appointed to the Albert Schweitzer Chair of the Humanities at the State University of New York at Albany.

Morrison's popularity burgeoned with the publication of *Beloved*, though she had already been making a name for herself as a respected novelist. Her readership and critical recognition have been growing steadily ever since the publication of *The Bluest Eye* (1970), her first novel. Her second novel, *Sula* (1974), was nominated for the 1975 National Book Award. With her third novel, *Song of Solomon* (1977), Morrison secured her place as an important black novelist, the book winning the National Book Critics Circle Award and the American Academy and Institute of Arts and Letters Award. Her fourth novel, *Tar Baby* (1981), made the bestseller list, and then six years later *Beloved* was released. Although nominated for the 1987 National Book Award and the National Book Critics Circle Award, *Beloved* was awarded neither, and, in response, 49 black writers published a protest letter in a *New York Times* advertisement. In 1988, however, *Beloved* won the prestigious Pulitzer Prize for fiction.

In 1989, Morrison became the Robert F. Goheen Professor in the Humanities at Princeton University, a position she continues to hold. Once, while giving a lecture at Princeton, Morrison was asked by a student "who she wrote for." She replied, "I want to write for people like me, which is to say black people, curious people, demanding people—people who can't be faked, people who don't need to be patronized, people who have very, very high criteria."

Morrison's success has continued to grow. In 1993, she was the first black woman to win the Nobel Prize for Literature. The Nobel Prize Foundation described her as one "who in novels characterized by visionary force and poetic import, gives life to an essential aspect of American reality." She also published two more novels: *Jazz* in 1992, and *Paradise* in 1998. Also in 1998, *Beloved* was adapted as a film, starring Oprah Winfrey as Sethe. To this day, Toni Morrison continues to employ her "high criteria" to challenge herself as both an educator and a writer. Her writing is at once difficult and accessible. She creates densely lyrical narratives that are instantly recognizable as her own, and she makes the particularity of the African-American experience the basis for her representation of humanity.

The Story Behind the Story

When she first began writing fiction, Toni Morrison did not believe she would become a writer. History has proven otherwise as Toni Morrison is recognized as one of the best known and most respected contemporary authors. Her work, though intentionally black, appeals to readers of all races and has earned a following from both scholars and the general public. Of her writing she has said, "I simply wanted to write literature that was irrevocably, indisputably black, not because its characters were, or because I was, but because it took as its creative task and sought as its credentials those recognized and verifiable principles of black art."

Before she was known as a writer, Toni Morrison worked as a successful senior editor at Random House Publishers specializing in black fiction. For many years she actively helped publish other black writers, and it was during this time that she stumbled across the inspiration for *Beloved*. While editing a project called *The Black Book* (1974), a compilation of memorabilia representing 300 years of black history, Morrison discovered the account of Margaret Garner. According to a newspaper article that Morrison had read, in 1851 Margaret Garner, a former slave, escaped with her children from Kentucky to Ohio. When her owner and a posse formed by the U.S. marshal in Cincinnati tracked her down, Garner threatened to kill her children crying out, "Before any of my children will be taken back into Kentucky, I will kill every one of them." Garner cut the throat of her three-year-old daughter before being restrained and eventually returned to Kentucky under the federal Fugitive Slave Law of 1850. Moved by the story, Morrison used Margaret Garner as a starting point for her story of Sethe, but she intentionally avoided further researching the Garner case, allowing Sethe to emerge as a fully-imagined character. Morrison spent about two years thinking on the plot and the characters for *Beloved*, and then took another three to write the book.

Toni Morrison was certain that *Beloved*, her fifth novel, would be the least read of all her works. She reasoned this because of the silent phenomenon she calls "national amnesia" that surrounds the history and details of slavery. She herself had felt reluctant to immerse herself in the subject, yet she was compelled to continue writing. To her surprise, *Beloved* appeared on the *New York Times* bestseller list the same week it appeared in bookstores.

List of Characters

Sethe (b. 1835), the protagonist of the novel, is a survivor of slavery. She escapes Sweet Home plantation and runs to Cincinnati to live with Baby Suggs, her mother-in-law. When her "master" comes to Cincinnati to reclaim Sethe and her children, Sethe cuts the throat of her youngest daughter and attempts to kill the others. The arrivals of Paul D and Beloved begin Sethe's emotional healing, as she tries to live in peace with her traumatic past.

Beloved is the name of the mysterious woman who arrives at 124 Bluestone Road. Beloved goes through various identities—an infant, a sister, a lover. Beloved represents the past and the slaves of the Middle Passage.

Denver (b. 1855) is Sethe's eighteen-year-old daughter. Solitary and imaginative, she clings to Beloved as a sister and companion. Born during Sethe's flight from Sweet Home to Cincinnati, Denver survives the scene of the infanticide and becomes the focus of Sethe's life.

Howard (b. 1850) and **Buglar** (b. 1851) are Sethe's sons. They run away from 124 Bluestone Road, afraid of the baby ghost.

Paul D is one of the Sweet Home men. He helps Sethe to survive and live with the painful memories of slavery.

Halle Suggs (b. 1835) is Sethe's husband, the father of her children, and the youngest of Baby Suggs's eight children.

Baby Suggs (1795—1865) is Halle's mother. She is also a spiritual leader in the black community. After Sethe kills her daughter, Baby Suggs gives up and disappears into her bedroom to "study color" until she dies.

Stamp Paid is the Kentucky slave who ferries Sethe and Denver across the Ohio River. When Sethe tries to kill her children, he saves Denver.

Amy Denver is the sixteen-year-old white indentured servant who runs away to Boston on a quest for "a piece of velvet." Amy finds Sethe pregnant, with her feet too swollen to walk. She massages Sethe's feet and helps her deliver Denver.

Mr. Garner is the mild-mannered master of Sweet Home. The fact that he treats his slaves "well" makes no difference in the fates of the Sweet Home men and Sethe.

Mrs. Lillian Garner is the wife of Mr. Garner. After her husband's death, she makes Schoolteacher the overseer of Sweet Home.

Schoolteacher is the widowed brother-in-law of Mr. Garner. After Mr. Garner dies, Schoolteacher is the cruel "master" of Sweet Home.

Sixo is one of the Sweet Home men. He is tied to a tree and burned alive by Schoolteacher after attempting to escape.

Ella is an agent of the Underground Railroad who escorts Sethe and the infant Denver to Baby Suggs' house. Ella isolates Sethe for committing infanticide but years later organizes a rescue to save Sethe from Beloved.

Lady Jones is the light-skinned teacher who conducts class in her home for the "unpicked children of Cincinnati." She helps to revive the community in providing for Sethe and Denver.

Edward Bodwin is a Quaker abolitionist and supporter of the Underground Railroad. He secures Sethe's release after her imprisonment and later offers Denver a job.

Summary and Analysis

Toni Morrison's *Beloved* explores the lasting effects of slavery on individual black men and women and their communities, and documents the destruction and resilient survival of the African people—60 million or more, according to Morrison's approximation of how many died in the Middle Passage. The narrative centers on Sethe, a former slave, and her struggle to move on from the past and embrace her freedom. Many critics have addressed how *Beloved* revises and revives the slave narrative tradition. While traditional slave narratives typically document the slave's physical escape and their journey to freedom, Morrison enriches this structure by depicting how the slaves survive the psychological trauma. "Memory, in *Beloved*," posits Marilyn Sanders Mobley, "revises the classical slave narratives by providing access to the sort of psychological integrity heretofore undocumented." (Mobley, 359) Bernard W. Bell adds, "Unlike the univocal, nineteenth-century slave narratives in which plot rides character in the protagonists' journey of transformation from object to subject, *Beloved* is a haunting story of a mother's love that frames a series of interrelated love stories ... by multiple narrators." (Bell, 10) Susan Bowers points out that most original authors of slave narratives did not reveal the true horror of slavery for fear of offending the white abolitionists, or because they themselves did not want to dwell on the painful memories. Bowers argues that Morrison's revision of the slave narrative "is one way of giving African Americans back their voices." (Bowers, 213) Furthermore, asserts critic Linda Krumholz, *Beloved* manages to focus on both the individual characters as well as the historical impact of slavery, exposing "slavery as a national trauma, and as an intensely personal trauma as well." (Krumholz, 396)

The novel's multiple and fragmented plot lines and shifting points of view create a layered and complex narrative structure. As Bell points out, this fragmented structure encourages the reader to interpret the characters' stories and fill in the gaps, "to reconstruct and reconsider the unspeakable human cost of American slavery, racism, and sexism, then and now ..." (Bell, 11).

Beloved consists of three formal parts, arranged into unnumbered chapters. In this analysis, however, numbers will be used in order to avoid confusion. Part One, beginning with Paul D's arrival at the house on Bluestone Road and ending with his departure, introduces motifs that will shape the major themes in the novel, including memory, motherhood, community, slavery, and freedom. Images and references introduced in Part One, such as the supernatural, the mammary rape of Sethe, and the "tree" on Sethe's back, begin to shape the characters' individual stories and memories.

The novel takes place during the period of Reconstruction (1870-90). **Chapter i** begins in 1873, eight years after the Civil War, near Cincinnati. The novel opens with the past literally haunting the present, uniting the uncanny with realism. Sethe and her daughter Denver are all that remain of the once-close family living in the "spiteful" house at 124 Bluestone Road. Nine years ago Sethe's two sons, Buglar and Howard, ran off, ostensibly in fear of the baby ghost, and shortly thereafter Baby Suggs dies.

Beloved does not follow a linear, chronological plot, but instead circles from past to present, with a series of flashbacks that gradually reveal the central characters' stories. In this first chapter, Sethe's thoughts revolve around her infant daughter, who now haunts the house. Sethe recalls that in exchange for the endearment "Beloved," to be chiseled into the grave marker, she had to have sex with the white stone cutter: "Ten minutes for seven letters." She wonders whether "Dearly" could have been added for "another ten." Now she lives in a house "palsied by the baby's fury at having its throat cut." The ghost causes trouble for the family, maiming the dog and upsetting furniture: "Who would have thought that a little old baby could harbor so much rage?"

Sethe once asked Baby Suggs if they should move out of the haunted home, and Baby Suggs replied that there was no point, that the shared grief of the black community was pervasive and infinite: "Not a house in the country ain't packed to its rafters with some dead Negro's grief. We lucky this ghost is a baby." The ghost is a symbol of the past, a reminder of the effects of slavery. Although the occupants of 124 are the first of a generation to be freed, they continue to live under slavery's destructive effects. The critic Karla Holloway, who considers *Beloved* to be a spiritual, explains that this "post-emancipation community" has been "nearly spiritually incapacitated by the trauma of slavery." (Holloway, 516)

Sethe's plan for survival revolves around remembering as little about the past as possible. She finds the process of memory, like the ghost of her baby girl, to be too painful, but her "brain [is] devious," and often the memories return without warning. For example, as she hurries across the field to get to the pump to rinse the chamomile sap from her legs, she sees, in a juxtaposition of the beauty of nature and the violent lynchings of black men, "Sweet Home rolling, rolling, rolling out before her eyes," with "boys hanging from the most beautiful sycamores in the world."

When Paul D, one of the Sweet Home men, shows up unexpectedly, the past becomes even more difficult to suppress. It has been 18 years since Sethe and Paul D have seen each other. Paul D's arrival provokes Sethe's memories and interrupts the routine of Sethe and Denver. Paul D immediately feels the presence of the ghost; he follows Sethe into the house and "straight into a pool of red and undulating light that locked him where he stood." He backs away, asking, "What kind of evil you got in here?" Sethe tells him the ghost is not evil, "just sad." Paul D recognizes this sadness: "a wave of grief soaked him so thoroughly he wanted to cry." The emotional effect the ghost has on Paul D reveals his sensitivity, while also symbolizing the pervasive haunting of the past. Critic Valerie Smith posits, "The characters have been so profoundly affected by the experience [of slavery] that time cannot separate them from its horrors or undo its effects." (Smith, 345) Although neither Sethe nor Paul D actively wants to remember the past, the emotions have taken root in their homes, bodies, and minds.

Sethe and Paul D's shared past revolves around Sweet Home, a Kentucky plantation, originally home to a white couple, Mr. and Mrs. Garner, and their slaves: Baby Suggs and her son Halle, Paul A, Paul D, Paul F, and Sixo. After Halle buys his mother out of slavery, the Garners replace Baby Suggs with thirteen-year-old Sethe.

As Sethe and Paul D share stories of Sweet Home, Denver feels left out of the conversation. Shy and lonely, she believes Paul D has infringed upon the intimate space between her and her mother. Denver, "lonely and rebuked" like the ghost, endures the effects of living in an isolated, haunted house where nobody has visited in twelve years. She mocks her mother and Paul D for reminiscing about the plantation, and Paul D admits, "It wasn't sweet and it sure wasn't home." Even with its painful memories, however, Sethe acknowledges that this was the only place they knew, and that the memory of being there "comes back whether we want it to or not."

The memories of Sweet Home include not only the Garners but also Schoolteacher, the cruel overseer who replaced Mr. Garner after his death. Mr. Garner, the original owner of Sweet Home, referred to his slaves as "men," as opposed to most slaveholders, who referred to their slaves as "boys." He also allowed his male slaves to carry guns, goading his neighbors with the "freedom" he gave them. When Schoolteacher replaced Garner after he died, however, Sweet Home dissolved into a nightmare of humiliation, beatings, and murders.

Sethe, tough and independent, claims she "will never run from another thing on this earth," and she tells Paul D that just before she escaped Sweet Home, Schoolteacher ordered his nephews to steal the milk from her breasts. The harrowing memory evokes the novel's motifs of motherhood, as Sethe is "treated like a sexually aggressive wet nurse and mammy" (Bouson, 141), while the perpetrators "[c]ruelly mock the maternal associations of nursing by treating Sethe as an animal to be milked."(Barnett, 422) For Sethe, this assault is a violation worse than the beating that followed, in which Schoolteacher's nephews violently whipped her, opening up her back and leaving a "tree" of scars to mark her. The "tree" is one of many physical reminders of the horror of slavery, and Paul D touches this place, "rub[s] his cheek on her back and learn[s] that way her sorrow, the roots of it; its wide trunk and intricate branches." For critic Susan Corey, the tree scar exemplifies the use of the grotesque: "[I]ts effect is both repulsive and attractive, signifying the complexity of Sethe's relationship to her past."(Corey, 34) Corey analyzes how the technique of the grotesque informs *Beloved*, defining the grotesque as "an aesthetic form that works through exaggeration, distortion, contradiction, disorder, and shock to disrupt a sense of normalcy and stimulate new meanings and connections" (32). For instance, when Sethe tells the story of this assault, the "scene shocks the reader with unspeakable horror and serves as a prime example of slavery's destructive effects on the imagination and the inner life" (34). The deformed skin signifies Sethe's futile hope to dull her memories, while also attesting to the permanent effect of the past. The "deadened nerves that alienate her from her bodily sensations" represent "the blocked memory and emotions that separate her from a full, subjective identity" (35). While the scar symbolizes the violence and horror of slavery, the blossoming "chokecherry tree" also plays on the natural beauty Sethe associates with Sweet Home.

When Paul D touches the scar and feels Sethe's sadness, the baby ghost reacts to their intimacy, causing the house to pitch and knock them around. Paul D tells the baby ghost to leave and in so doing exorcises the ghost from the house. Paul D and Sethe make love in **chapter ii**, and immediately afterwards their desire disappears. They lay in bed with their separate memories and thoughts distancing them from each other. This chapter begins to reveal more about Sethe and Paul D's individual pasts at Sweet Home, while also describing the destructive forces of slavery, on both families and individuals. Sethe thinks about Baby Suggs, for example, a survivor of the Middle Passage. Baby Suggs had been moved from plantation to plantation, sold and resold, separated from all of her children, until she was placed at Sweet Home with her son Halle. Slavery controlled sexuality, as it did all other aspects of humanity and identity:

"Men and women were moved around like checkers." Baby Suggs's eight children were fathered by six different men, and anyone she had loved "who hadn't run off or been hanged, got rented out, loaned out, brought up, brought back, stored up, mortgaged, won, stolen or seized." Sethe's life was different; she and Halle were married for six years, although now Sethe remembers Halle more as a brother than a husband.

Paul D also recalls Sweet Home and its effect on intimate relationships. His memories revolve around his slave-brother Sixo, the only one of the slave men who actively resisted slavery. He did not allow anyone to choose a mate for him. Instead he sneaked away from Sweet Home at night to meet with a woman of his own choosing while the rest of the men lusted after Sethe and satisfied themselves with farm animals.

In **chapter iii**, Denver, lonely because her mother and Paul D are catching up on old times, takes refuge in her secret hiding place under the canopy of the boxwood hedge. Although Denver was born free, she too is enslaved—by the isolation of the house and her mother's haunted memories. Denver has not left the property of 124 since she was a young child. The baby ghost has been her only playmate. Denver does not like to listen to stories from her mother's past, though she does find comfort in the story of her own birth. This is the only story from Sethe's past that Denver likes to hear, because the story not only includes her, but also gestures of hope and kindness.

Through this story the reader begins to learn about Sethe's escape from Sweet Home. Nine months pregnant and on the run, Sethe reaches the Ohio River with her feet badly swollen. She is saved by a white girl, Amy Denver, a sixteen-year-old indentured servant who is on her way to Boston to buy "some velvet." This scene with Amy depicts one of the few acts of kindness by a white person, as Amy tries to minister to Sethe: "[she] lifted Sethe's feet and legs and massaged them until [Sethe] cried salt tears." Denver remembers the details of the story as if it is her own "rememory," those pictures of the mind "never going away."

During the course of **chapter iv** tension escalates between Denver and Paul D, and Sethe warns Paul D she will not "hear a word against" her daughter. Paul D believes Sethe's protective nature and immense love for her children represent a dangerous risk: "[F]or a used-to-be-slave woman to love anything that much was dangerous, especially if it was her children she had settled on to love." Paul D believes the only way to stop the past from overtaking him is to "love just a little bit." Although Paul D promises to be there for Sethe, he cannot truly commit to her until he faces and accepts the past—both his and hers. However, he hopes to show Sethe and Denver his desire to take care of them by treating them to the carnival. For the duration of that evening, even Denver is happy with Paul D. The familial intimacy is symbolized in the image Sethe notices: "[T]he shadows of three people still held hands."

When Denver, Paul D, and Sethe return from the carnival, in the beginning of **chapter v**, they see an exhausted, well-dressed woman sitting outside of 124. She tells them her name is Beloved. Upon seeing the woman, Sethe immediately has to relieve herself, an uncontrollable gush of water that alludes to her water breaking and symbolizes the (re)birth of her deceased daughter. The woman is thirsty and sleepy, her voice "low and rough." Images of infancy surround Beloved: her neck seems unable to support her head, her skin is soft and unlined, and she drinks as greedily as a nursing infant. She is sick with "croup." Under Denver's watchful care, Beloved sleeps in Baby Suggs's bed for four days, and when she finally fully opens her dreamy, slit eyes, Denver is startled: "[D]own in those big black eyes there was no expression at all." The description of her eyes echoes an earlier description of Sethe's eyes as eyes that "did not pick up a flicker of light." Beloved also has an extreme sweet tooth, like a child, and she is too weak to walk on her own—although Paul D sees her pick up the rocker with one hand.

Four weeks later (**chapter vi**), Beloved hovers around Sethe "like a familiar." Sethe, flattered by Beloved's devotion, "licked, tasted, eaten by Beloved's eyes," tells the childlike woman stories in order "to feed her." Beloved craves Sethe's memories as she does sweets. Although the past has the tendency to hurt Sethe "like a tender place in the corner of her mouth that a bit left," when she tells the stories to Beloved, she "found herself wanting to, liking it." Beloved knows intimate details about Sethe that a stranger could not possibly know, mentioning, for example, Sethe's "diamond" earrings; her familiar knowledge of Sethe's past adds more mystery to Beloved.

When Beloved asks about Sethe's mother, Sethe reports that she hardly knew her mother. Her mother worked in the fields, while Nan, a one-armed wet nurse, acted as Sethe's surrogate mother. Her mother was lynched when Sethe was only a child, and she remembers trying to identify the body by her mother's "mark," another reference to the physical scars of slavery. Sethe also recalls that her mother spoke in a different language "which would never come back"—one of many references in *Beloved* that illustrates slavery's attempt to rob slaves of their native African culture. Although Beloved stirs up Sethe's emotional pain, she is also a catalyst for bringing forth Sethe's repressed memories, and Sethe finds herself "remembering something she had forgotten she knew." Although she can no longer remember her mother's native language, she now remembers Nan's "message." Sethe's mother, Nan told her, had been raped many times by the white crew of the Middle Passage, and she "threw away" these babies. Sethe's mother kept her because she was the child of a black man, whom her mother had "put her arms around." Sethe's memory of her mother evokes important themes of motherhood: how did slavery threaten to destroy the bonds between mothers and children? Sethe's tenuous relationship with her own mother, who was nearly a stranger to her, might also help explain her own protective, needy love toward her children.

Beloved greedily feeds on Sethe's stories in **chapter vii** yet reveals nothing about herself. Paul D finds this unsettling and begins to resent how she has come into their lives. He does not like the way she is "shining" toward Sethe and suspects there is some significance to the timing of Beloved's arrival, just when the three of them were starting to feel like a family. He asks her where she came from and how she got there, and she answers, cryptically, that she came from a place a "long, long, long, long way. Nobody bring me. Nobody help me."

Sethe defends her reason to allow Beloved to stay, telling Paul D he could never understand "how it feels to be a colored woman roaming the roads with anything God made liable to jump on you." This statement leads them into a conversation about Halle, who Sethe believes betrayed her and the children. Yet as Paul D and Sethe put their stories together, they surmise that Halle must have witnessed Schoolteacher's nephews assaulting Sethe. This would explain why the last time Paul D saw Halle he was sitting by the churn with "butter all over his face." Paul D confesses to Sethe that he could not help his friend because he was chained with a bit in his mouth. The image stirs up their anger and humiliation and pain. Sethe remembers the "mossy-teethed" boys holding her down and sucking her milk as Schoolteacher watched and took notes, and now she must enlarge this vicious memory to include the image of her husband gone mad.

Paul D recalls his own humiliation under the gaze of Mister, the plantation's rooster: "Schoolteacher changed me. I was something else and that something was less than a chicken sitting in the sun on a tub." As the rooster roamed freely, Paul D was chained with a bit in his mouth, a memory he had never spoken aloud until now. He stops himself from saying anything more, wanting to keep his past "in that tobacco tin buried in his chest where a red heart used to be." Sethe sympathizes with his desire to quiet the past. Her own method of survival follows the rule of the "day's serious work of beating back the past."

Both Sethe and Paul D are trauma victims, and one way to deal with their horrors involves repressing painful memories. Although Sethe and Paul D attempt to suppress the past, it emerges in broken threads and pieces, and these memories eventually allow them to come to terms with the trauma they suffered. What Sethe terms "rememory" moves the narrative back and forth between past and present; it is a way to reconstruct what has been forgotten, or, as Bowers explains, "memory escalates its battle against amnesia" (Bowers, 214).

Bouson describes "rememory" as "uncontrolled remembering and reliving of emotionally painful experiences," (Bouson, 135) and Krumholz analyzes how "rememory" becomes the characters' "central ritual of healing." (Krumholz, 396)

While Paul D and Sethe share the intimacy of their memories together in **chapter viii**, Denver craves a similar intimacy with Beloved. She asks her, "What's it like over there, where you were born?" and Beloved describes a "hot" place: "A lot of people is down there. Some is dead." Beloved's mysterious answer could suggest the womb or perhaps a grave. For Denver, the answer confirms her belief that Beloved is her dead sister, returned in the flesh. At Beloved's request, Denver gladly recites the story of her own birth, again evoking her mother's memory. Denver begins to imagine her mother through the eyes of Beloved, and the story becomes "a duet as they lay down together, Denver nursing Beloved's interest like a lover whose pleasure was to overfeed the loved." Morrison again transports the reader back to the scene with Sethe, near death and pregnant, and the white girl, Amy Denver. Together these "two lawless outlaws" deliver the free baby into the world. Denver is born in a boat with the Ohio River's water washing over her—representing the first generation of freedom. After Denver is born, Amy Denver resumes her quest to Boston for a piece of velvet, and Sethe, exhausted and feverish, prepares to cross the Ohio River. Sethe's escape from Sweet Home, and the infant to whom she has just given birth, represent her own resistance to slavery's attempt to control black motherhood.

In **chapter ix**, Morrison begins to contrast the house from the in twenty-eight days of Sethe's happiness, when she was reunited with her children and mother-in-law, and its current state. During the first days of Sethe's arrival, 124 "had been a cheerful, buzzing house where Baby Suggs, holy, loved, cautioned, fed, chastised, and soothed." The house represented a welcoming center and Baby Suggs its "unchurched preacher," ministering to the community because she "had nothing left to make a living with but her heart—which she put to work at once."

Baby Suggs's preaching ignores and subverts conventional Christian doctrines and practices; instead of a church she leads her followers to the "Clearing" in the forest, a place which "signifies the necessity for a psychological cleansing of the past, a space to encounter painful memories safely and rest from them." (Krumholz, 397) Critic Nancy Jesser describes the Clearing as "a space outside the political and cultural domain of the white people who constantly disturb the black community of Cincinnati." (Jesser, 332) Hence, the Clearing becomes a space for the black community to claim their own space for spiritual healing and community building. Here Baby Suggs encourages her congregation to love themselves and their children. She does not condemn them or frighten them: "She did not tell them to clean up their lives or to go and sin no more. She did not tell them they were the blessed of the earth, its inheriting meek or its glory bound pure. She told them that the only grace they could have was the grace they could imagine. That if they could not see it, they would not have it." Baby Suggs's language focuses on the physical: she instructs her congregation to sing, dance, and cry. She wants them to love their hands, their flesh, and their hearts, stressing that only by fully loving themselves will they find freedom. She reminds the people of what the world thinks of them: "Yonder they do not love your flesh. They despise it." Her preaching helps to heal their broken spirits, to "restore the bodies of those battered by their enslavement." (Smith, 346)

Missing the spirituality and strength of Baby Suggs, Sethe takes Denver and Beloved to the Clearing to "pay tribute to Halle." The narrative once again circles back to the story of Denver's birth. Sethe, exhausted and ill, meets Stamp Paid, a conductor for the Underground Railroad—a system of safe houses that hid and supported slaves until they could reach "free" states or Canada. Stamp Paid ferries her across the Ohio River to freedom. Another one of the Railroad's agents, a young woman named Ella, brings news to Sethe that Stamp Paid has already safely brought Sethe's three children to 124 Bluestone. Then, for the first time, Sethe meets Baby Suggs, and she is reunited with her children.

During those twenty-eight days, Sethe experiences the freedom of "unslaved life." She becomes a part of the community and, as an expression of this new freedom, she proclaims: "Freeing yourself was one thing; claiming ownership of that free self was another." During those twenty-eight days of freedom, Sethe is welcomed by and engages with the community; it is a period that contrasts with the present state: "[T]here was no one, for they would not visit her while the baby ghost filled the house, and she returned their disapproval with the potent pride of the mistreated." As Sethe remembers these times and considers the possibility of a new life with Paul D, invisible fingers, which she assumes belong to Baby Suggs, caress her neck. Baby Suggs had healed Sethe once before. When she first arrived at 124, the gentle Baby Suggs washed her, ministering to her torn back the way Amy Denver had cared for her feet, both scenes evoking the theme of the healing power of flesh. Baby Suggs understood the way to heal was through touch, and critic Valerie Smith draws the conclusion, "The project of the novel, much like Baby Suggs's project, seems to be to reclaim these bodies, to find a way to tell the story of the slave body in pain." (Smith, 348)

However, these invisible fingers suddenly strengthen, leaving bruises around Sethe's neck. Denver knows the hurtful fingers do not belong to Baby Suggs, and later she accuses Beloved of choking her mother. Beloved argues, "I kissed her neck. I didn't choke it. The circle of iron choked it." The "circle of iron" refers to the iron collar, used to humiliate and physically control slaves, another reminder of slavery and its marks on the body.

Although her mother's "rememory" and the retelling of the story of her birth seem to dominate Denver's mind, Denver also has her own specific memories of the past. For instance, she remembers she did not always stay within the property of 124. When she was seven years old, she took school lessons with Lady Jones. However, these outings were put to a stop when a fellow classmate made it clear to her why her family was shunned, "Didn't your mother get locked away for murder? Wasn't you in there with her when she went?" After this confrontation, Denver not only stopped socializing with the world outside of 124, but also went deaf. Fearful of hearing more about her mother, she "walked in a silence too solid for penetration," yet the deafness gave her "eyes a power even she found hard to believe." Critics have pointed out that Denver suffers her mother's trauma. Denver "is as trapped by Sethe's past as Sethe is," (Krumholz, 404) states Krumholz, while Bouson asserts that "trauma and shame are contagious and can be transmitted from parent to child" (Bouson, 155). Denver's deafness stays with her for two years, until the arrival of the baby ghost.

Chapter x focuses on Paul D's journey after he leaves Sweet Home. Whereas Sethe's journey had a concrete purpose—to be reunited with her children—Paul D's journey became a way to wander and put the past far behind him. As with Sethe's experiences, the narrative presents Paul D's life after Sweet Home in a series of flashbacks. Although he copes by shrinking his emotions, locking them away in the "tobacco tin," his violent, hurtful memories of the eighty-six days he spent on the chain gang in Alfred, Georgia, reemerge. Like the other prisoners, Paul D was locked in a small box "like a cage," beaten and humiliated, and sexually assaulted by the white prison guards. Critic Pamela Barnett cites this sexual assault as one of the most painful memories Paul D locks in his box, and she suggests that Paul D "cannot speak of that experience in a language that does not account for the sexually victimized male body or that casts that body as feminized." (Barnett, 424)

While on the chain gang, the only way the men can confront the horror of their situation is through "call and response." The leader issues a "call," the group responds, and then the leader issues a new call that incorporates the initial communal response, and a new cycle begins. This technique becomes a means of survival, both figuratively and literally. As the men worked they "beat" on life, "sang it out and beat it up, garbling the words so they would not be understood; trickling the words so their syllables yielded up other meanings." The men, bound by the chain looped through their ankle cuffs, are also connected by something deeper—the power of community. All of them recognize that "a man could risk his own life, but not his brother's." The men escape while chained together: a tug on the chain sends the message to the next man, creating a physical type of call and response, and in the confusion and danger of a flood and mudslide, the prisoners escape. They spend several weeks with a group of Cherokee Indians, themselves fugitives from U.S. soldiers, and then Paul D heads north on his own, following "the tree flowers" to freedom. He stays with a woman in Delaware for eighteen months, hardening his heart, "the tobacco tin lodged in his chest," and wanders until he reunites with Sethe.

Upon arriving at Sethe's home, Paul D has hopes of making a life with Sethe, but Beloved's arrival interferes with this plan. In **chapter xi**, Beloved gains emotional power over Paul D Restless, he moves from room to room in the house, trying to find a place to sleep and to cut himself off from his desire and her seduction. He moves out into the shed, and she shows up on his door and tells him, "I want you to touch me on the inside part and call me my name." Paul D calls out, "Red heart. Red heart. Red heart," his tobacco chest finally being broken open as he touches Beloved.

Most critics agree that having sex with Beloved is an important catalyst for Paul D, allowing him to connect with his body, emotions, and memories. For example, critic Susan Bowers asserts, "When Beloved seduces Paul D, making love with her breaks open the tobacco tin in his chest to release his red heart." (Bowers, 217) Susan Corey believes "these sexual encounters are important for Paul D's recovery of self." (Corey, 39) Pamela Barnett, however, reads this scene differently, calling Beloved a "succubus" figure—an African American folklore demon that sexually assaults male victims. Paul D, in Barnett's reading, is "a victim of a supernatural rape that he feels has emasculated him just as the guards in Alfred, Georgia did." (Barnett, 424) Barnett also agrees that this rape forces Paul D to re-experience the previous sexual assault in Alfred, Georgia, and eventually leads to healing: "without this nightmare experience, Paul D would not be able to overcome his numbing defense mechanisms." (423)

Throughout the novel, each of the main characters—Sethe, Paul D, and Denver—responds to Beloved differently. For example, Bowers suggests that in relating to Beloved, each character "addresses her or his most profound individual anguish, whatever lies at the core of each identity. For Sethe, it is mothering; for Paul D, his ability to feel; and for Denver, her loneliness. Their individual reactions to her reflect their respective voids and reveal their deepest selves." (Bowers, 216) As Part I follows the three characters' relationships with Beloved and the effect she has over their own development, Beloved goes through several incarnations in the novel; she acts as an infant, a sexual woman, a daughter, and a sister.

Like Paul D, Denver is also seduced by Beloved in **chapter xii**, relishing the moments when Beloved "rested cheek on knuckles and looked at Denver with attention." Although her mother believes Beloved was "locked up by some white man for his own purposes, and never let out of the door," Denver believes "Beloved was the white dress that had knelt with her mother in the keeping room, the true-to-life presence of the baby that had kept her company for most of her life." Denver's life has been marked by loss—her brothers, her grandmother, her father—and she "won't put up with another leaving, another trick." As with the other characters, Beloved has both a positive, healing effect on Denver and also a potentially damaging one. Fearful that Beloved has disappeared, for example, Denver cries "because she has no self."

One of the themes in **chapter xiii** addresses Paul D's struggle to regain his manhood. The chapter begins with a memory of Sweet Home, and Paul D again reflects how Mr. Garner called them men: "[T]hey were believed and trusted, but most of all they were listened to," and Schoolteacher "taught them otherwise." When Garner died, the illusion of the slaves' freedom died with him. "Garner's model farm places his slaves in a false position of community" (Jesser, 327), critic Nancy Jesser explains, and in the end "this allowed manhood does not change the basic relationship of owned and owner" (328). Although Garner might have referred to them as "men," once they stepped off his property "they were trespassers among the human race." Schoolteacher makes this sentiment all too well known, treating the men like chattel. Paul D struggles with his concept of masculinity, realizing that the institution of slavery does not allow for "men."

Paul D also feels "shame," fearful that Beloved has challenged and undermined his manhood: "A grown man fixed by a girl? But what if the girl was not a girl, but something in disguise?" He thinks he will tell Sethe the truth, but when he sees her he cannot tell her, "I am not a man." Instead he blurts out that he wants her to be pregnant: "And suddenly it was a solution: a way to hold on to her, document his manhood and break out of the girl's spell—all in one." Pamela Barnett believes this statement indicates that Paul D's "shame is too great, and rather than ask for help he reverts to anxious assertions of his masculinity." (Barnett, 424) Later, at the supper table, Sethe tells Paul D she wants him to begin sleeping with her now. However, Sethe doesn't want to be pregnant, and she suspects Paul D only wants this baby so that he can be a part of the threesome—the family consisting of Sethe, Denver, and Beloved.

Beloved worries that Paul D is coming between her and Sethe in **chapter xiv**. In one of the few moments when the narrator moves into Beloved's perspective, the reader learns her fear of "exploding and being swallowed." Beloved pulls out one of her teeth and worries: "Next would be her arm, her hand, a toe. Pieces of her would drop maybe one at a time, maybe all at once." This scene foreshadows the destruction that is to come and acknowledges Beloved's dependence on others. For survival, she must swallow pieces of the other characters; otherwise she will literally dissolve.

Baby Suggs, although dead, is brought back into the narrative in **chapter xv** to recall her joy over the arrival of Sethe and her children, and her anguish over her son Halle, who she assumes is dead. Baby Suggs remembers how Stamp Paid stopped by with pails of sweet, succulent blackberries, and from there a feast began. However, the feast's "mood of joy is diminished by the allusions to the Last Supper with its overtones of betrayal, suffering, and tragic death—of sorrow mixed with joy." (Corey, 41) The feast also represents the divisions of class within the black community, as the community "ate so well, and laughed so much, it made them angry." The next morning Baby Suggs senses something in the air and realizes "her friends and neighbors were angry at her because she had overstepped, given too much, offended them by excess." The community makes assumptions about Baby Suggs's prosperity and freedom, and their resentment leads to passivity: by not warning Baby Suggs of the approaching horsemen, the community fails to protect her family. The novel stresses the importance of community, of sharing collective memories and healing each other, and with this breakdown of solidarity, Baby Suggs and her family become vulnerable to the approaching doom.

This doom reveals itself in **chapter xvi** as the "four horsemen," an allusion to the four horsemen in Revelation, cites Susan Bowers, who reads the novel as an apocalyptic work (Bowers, 221). Schoolteacher has come to take Sethe and her children back into slavery, an action that was legal under the Fugitive Slave Act of 1850, which stated that runaway slaves could be reclaimed even from a free state.

Morrison flattens this climactic scene, making it even more shocking. For example, by focusing on Biblical references, J. Brooks Bouson posits, the narrative builds up the atmosphere of doom and deflects "reader attention from the horror of the central scene that is to unfold—the infanticide." (Bouson, 144) The narrative also switches viewpoints, positioning the reader in the perspective of Schoolteacher. The readers are relocated "within the shaming perspective of the racist white onlooker," and this technique creates another level of tension. (Bouson, 145) The reader is uncomfortable and shocked as the scene unfolds. Now, through the perspective of Schoolteacher, Sethe, the protagonist, is described to the reader as a "nigger woman holding a blood-soaked child to her chest." Schoolteacher, whom Susan Bowers considers the Antichrist figure. (Bowers, 220) shows no sympathy for the dead and is only irritated that he has lost his "property": "Right off it was clear, to schoolteacher especially, that there was nothing there to claim." Schoolteacher does not claim Sethe, as he believes that she is crazy for killing her child. He does not realize that Sethe loves her children so much that she would rather kill them than allow them to be dehumanized by slavery.

The narrative has revealed Sethe's story in fragments, giving the reader the opportunity to interpret and piece together the parts. As "Sethe modifies, amplifies, and subverts her own memory of the murder that serves as the locus of the narrative" (Mobley, 360), suspense and tension build. **Chapter xvii** retells Sethe's act of infanticide from Stamp Paid's point of view. Now the reader is privy to witnessing Sethe's terror, how she ran through the yard "snatching up her children like a hawk on the wing." The narrative then returns to the present, with Stamp Paid showing Paul D the newspaper clipping that describes Sethe's crime. Paul D, who cannot read, rejects the truth, arguing the picture is not her: "That ain't her mouth."

Although Paul D refuses to believe this story, Sethe convinces him that it is true. In **chapter xviii**, Sethe is allowed for the first time to express her own repressed memory of the day. However, she has trouble articulating the story. Instead she explains how much she loved and protected her children, the story circles making Paul D "dizzy." Sethe's first priority has always been her children, she insists, as she talks about freedom and her "big" love for her children, and her initial happiness at 124. Paul D starts to understand: "He knew exactly what she meant: to get to a place where you could love anything you chose—not to need permission for desire—well now, *that* was freedom." Sethe circles the subject only because for her "the truth was simple." On that frightful day, she had recognized Schoolteacher's hat as the four horsemen approached, and the "hummingbirds stuck their needle beaks right though her headcloth into her hair and beat their wings. And if she thought anything, it was No. No. Nono. Nonono. Simple." She finishes by telling Paul that she successfully "stopped" Schoolteacher from taking her children, and Paul hears "a roaring" in his head. "Your love is too thick," he accuses. "Love is or it ain't," she replies; "thin love ain't love at all." She believes that her love "worked," that at least her children are not at Sweet Home with Schoolteacher, but Paul D cannot accept this part of her past. He judges her, telling her what she did was wrong: "You got two feet, Sethe, not four." Although Paul D may pass judgment on Sethe, Morrison never judges Sethe's murder or the community's response to this act, and this aspect of the narrative contributes to its haunting effect.

Part Two marks the shift in the reader's position from incomplete to complete knowledge of Sethe's act of infanticide. Furthermore, the stories of Denver's birth and Paul D's past in Alfred, Georgia, have reached completion. Part Two also builds on Sethe's present relationship with Beloved. The narrative in **chapter ix** switches between Stamp Paid and Sethe. Stamp blames himself for Paul D's departure, and he approaches 124 to make amends, thinking specifically of Baby Suggs and "the honor that was her due." He considers how the black community failed Baby Suggs, and how their isolation of Baby Suggs's family continued even after her death, so that Baby Suggs, "having devoted her freed life to harmony, was buried amid a regular dance of pride, fear, condemnation and spite." Sethe's fierce pride and independence, and her refusal to show remorse for the murder, also contribute to the family's isolation. *Beloved* juxtaposes the strength of community—such as in the Clearing gatherings with Baby Suggs—with the isolation of the individual, as illustrated by the change in 124 to a haunted, lonely place.

As Stamp Paid pauses at the front door, the loud, strange voices coming from the house stop him from knocking. The speech sounds like "something was wrong with the order of the words" and the only word he can decipher is "mine." He cannot bring himself to knock, a gesture that would acknowledge that he has become "a stranger at the gate"— whereas once he considered himself a close relation to Baby Suggs and her family. Now he feels tired, the way Baby Suggs must have felt "when she lay down and thought about color for the rest of her life." Stamp shamefully remembers how he was angry at her for not continuing to preach the Word. When he tried to convince her to go on, she continued to repeat, "I'm saying they came in my yard," and he realizes now that the "whitefolks had tired her out at last." After Sethe killed her daughter, Baby Suggs gave up and lay down in her bed, no longer a part of the community. She instead spent her last days studying colors, so that she could "fix on something harmless in this world." Colors, unlike whites, she claimed, "don't hurt nobody."

The narrative moves deeper into Stamp's thoughts, and into the history of slavery and its after effects—the KKK, lynchings, whippings. For Stamp Paid, the history and horror of slavery are symbolized in the ribbon he finds in the water, "knotted around a curl of wet woolly hair, clinging to its bit of scalp," which he carries around with him as a reminder of the past and its indescribable horror. As the voices culminate in 124, he believes these are the cries of the "people of the broken necks, of fire-cooked blood and black girls who had lost their ribbons. What a roaring." These voices symbolize the inadequacy of language in describing slavery. There are no clear words, only the "roaring," made up of "the mumbling of the black and angry dead" mixed in with "the thoughts of the women of 124, unspeakable thoughts, unspoken."

In the early part of the chapter Sethe resigns herself to living a life alone with her children. She realizes those "twenty-eight happy days were followed by eighteen years of disapproval and a solitary life" until the arrival of Paul D. Yet now she must let go of the brief time of "sun-splashed life" with him and devote her energy to Beloved and Denver.

Back at the house, after a playful afternoon of ice-skating, "the click [comes]" and Sethe realizes Beloved's true identity. She accepts Beloved, the representation of her innermost desire, as the reincarnation of her murdered daughter. Sethe now feels that Paul D tried to trick her, encouraging her to think about a different world, so that she did not even recognize her own daughter. Now she knows "[t]he world is in this room. This here's all there is and all there needs to be." She revises an earlier image of the three shadows holding hands until she believes that the hands belonged to her and her two daughters, not Paul D.

Sethe hopes that with the return of Beloved she will no longer have to remember or explain, because Beloved "understands it all." However, for the rest of the novel, she will try relentlessly to explain to Beloved why she killed her, begging for forgiveness. Although Sethe wants to be "wrapped in a timeless present," her memory returns to the past, as she considers the crimes that white people have committed against her and her loved ones. "Once, long ago, she was soft, trusting" of white people, but now that has changed after years of witnessing the terror inflicted upon her and her people. She had tried to keep these memories at bay, until "Paul D dug it up, gave her back her body, kissed her divided back, stirred her rememory and bought her more news: of clabber, or iron, or roosters' smiling, but when he heard *her* news, he counted her feet and didn't even say good-bye."

Paul D's condemnation of her, as having "four feet," evokes one of Sethe's most painful memories at Sweet Home, a memory that she did not share with Paul D, just as he did not tell her about the sexual assault in Alfred, Georgia. One day at Sweet Home she overheard Schoolteacher teaching his nephews about her, instructing them to make a list with "her human characteristics on the left; her animal ones on the right. And don't forget to line them up." Schoolteacher measures the slaves' skulls, making "scientific" inquiries. He is a practitioner of the nineteenth-century "science" of race, writing a book that attempts to "prove" his racist theories of white supremacy. He even watches and takes notes as his nephews milk Sethe as if she were an animal. Sethe, however, resists and rejects his dangerous, racist definitions. Bell argues that Sethe has a "black feminist sense of self-sufficiency." (Bell, 9) Now Sethe feels compelled to put all of this behind her, as she returns home from work to a house that "wasn't lonely-looking anymore."

Chapter xx is the first of four chapters that use the technique of stream of consciousness, a structure, Holloway explains, that enables the narrative to "emerge as an introspective that unfolds the dimensions of both the mind and history in a visually rich and dazzling projection of a revisioned time and space." (Holloway, 518) This chapter focuses on

Sethe's first-person account of Beloved's return: "But my love was tough and she back now." Sethe remembers the past in short explosive images, reiterating that she wanted to kill her children in order to "save" them from the horror of slavery. She recalls being forced to give up her child's milk, the milk a symbol of motherhood, thereby evoking the absence of her own mother: "I know what it is to be without the milk that belongs to you; to have to fight and holler for it, and to have so little left."

Beloved examines the complexity of love—the lack of it, which leads to destruction, and the "thick" love that threatens to engulf a person. Sethe's love for Beloved is both a desire to possess and a life-sustaining substance: "[W]hen I tell you you mine, I also mean I'm yours. I wouldn't draw breath without my children." Critic Trudier Harris points out the danger of her excessive love, and also the complexity of motherhood: "In carving out a definition of motherhood in a world where she had no models for that status, in shaping a concept of love from a void, Sethe has erred on the side of excess, a destructive excess that inadvertently gives primacy to the past and death rather than to life and the future."(Harris, 339) Sethe wrongly believes that with the return of Beloved, she has found peace, and now she "can sleep like the drowned."

"Beloved is my sister. I swallowed her blood right along with my mother's milk," Denver states in **chapter xxi**, as she remembers the day that Sethe murdered the baby and held Denver to her nipple, forcing her to swallow both her mother's milk and her sister's blood. This powerful image symbolizes the bond of motherhood, and also the danger of excess loving; just as Denver swallows the blood that results from her mother's crime, she embodies her mother's trauma by carrying the guilt inside of her. Denver now admits she spent much of her childhood afraid of her mother, who "killed one of her own daughters." Denver understands her brothers left not only because of the ghost but also because their mother had attempted to kill them. From the first time she saw her, Denver has believed that Beloved is the reincarnation of her sister, and she wants to protect her from Sethe: "Maybe it's still in her the thing that makes it all right to kill her children." Denver also considers her father, whom she never met, and she waits for his return: "I spent all of my outside self loving Ma'am so she wouldn't kill me, loving her even when she braided my head at night. I never let her know my daddy was coming for me." In contradiction to Sethe's idea of her family as consisting of her and her two daughters, for Denver, her family consists of her, her sister, and her father.

Beloved gets the opportunity to tell her story in **chapter xxii**. This section contains one certain statement by Beloved: "I am beloved and she is mine." This chapter, told from Beloved's point of view, is constructed in choppy sentences, without use of punctuation, and provides ambiguous images relating to her background. Critics often point out how the chapter's structure reflects Beloved's state of being. Marilyn Mobley interprets the "[l]iteral spaces between groups of words" as signaling "the timelessness of her presence as well as the unlived spaces of her life." (Mobley, 362)

Beloved's narrative hints at her existence among the dead, yet also strongly suggests that she remembers being a part of the Middle Passage. She recalls being with her mother, who was picking flowers from the leaves, the only peaceful image in this narrative. Other images and phrases, such as the "circle around her neck" and "storms rock us," suggest that she is describing being aboard a ship. She remembers her mother jumping into the water, abandoning her, and escaping. In this section she takes on the identity of a survivor of the Middle Passage. Further descriptions, such as "he hurts where I sleep" and "there is a house," suggest Beloved could be a real person, as opposed to a ghost, who has lived a secluded life in slavery.

"I am Beloved and she is mine" begins **chapter xxiii**. In this chapter more of Beloved's narrative is revealed. She believes Sethe "was about to smile at me when the men without skin came and took us up into the sunlight with the dead." She is convinced that "Sethe went into the sea. She went there. They did not push her. She went there." Beloved believes now she has found her mother, whom she believes to be Sethe, and this time she will not lose her, this time "she is [hers]." In this chapter, the narrative seems to shift into a dialogue of questions and answers between different voices. This section evokes themes of ownership, identity, and love. By the end of the section, the voices merge into a chorus, blurring as one:

Beloved
You are my sister
You are my daughter
You are my face; you are me
I have found you again; you have come back to me
You are my Beloved
You are mine
You are mine
You are mine

These final lines of repetition symbolize the characters' need for Beloved: she symbolizes hopes and desires, and holding onto her represents a way to survive.

Is Beloved a ghost, a real person, or a symbol? Many critics have analyzed her character, reaching different but often overlapping interpretations. Susan Corey calls Beloved one of the novel's most obvious forms of the grotesque. She explains that Beloved resembles an African river goddess, a potentially dangerous spirit because of her unnatural death. (Corey, 37)

Many critics believe Beloved symbolizes the ghost of Sethe's daughter, as well as the ghost of slavery. Critic Pamela Barnett asserts that Beloved evokes memory: "Beloved represents African American history or collective memory as much as she does Sethe's or Paul D's individual memory." (Barnett, 420) Susan Bowers writes that Beloved represents "the collective unconscious of African Americans," and she is an "embodiment of the collective pain and rage of millions of slaves who died on the Middle Passage." (Bowers, 217) Karla Holloway posits: "If Beloved is not only Sethe's dead daughter returned, but the return of all faces, all the drowned, but remembered, faces of mothers and their children who have lost their being because of the force of the EuroAmerican slave history, then she has become a cultural mooring place, a moment for reclamation and for naming." (Holloway, 522)

Critics also differ in how they gauge Beloved's dangerous side. Although Beloved "promotes a healing and growth for Sethe and Paul D, both of whom have closed off their emotional lives following their traumatic past experiences," she is also dangerous, Susan Corey points out, as evidenced in her need to possess Sethe completely (Corey, 37). While critic Pamela Barnett focuses on Beloved as a demon, Nancy Krumholz is quick to point out that "Beloved embodies the suffering and guilt of the past, but she also embodies the power and beauty of the past and the need to realize the past fully in order to bring forth the future, pregnant with possibilities." (Krumholz, 401)

Thus, Beloved has provoked many powerful interpretations. Her identity is not fixed; she is alternately a daughter, a sister, and a lover. While often representing what the characters desire her to be, she also symbolizes the past—individual pasts, as well as the collective history of slavery. While forcing characters to remember the horror of slavery by bringing forth suppressed memories and emotions, she also threatens to drown the characters in that past. Beloved is both a healer and a destroyer, her arrival both necessary and troubling.

For example, Paul D's consummation with Beloved has made him recall the past so vividly that he must now face the truth (**chapter xxiv**). The tobacco tin has "blown open, spilled contents that floated freely and made him their play and prey." After Sethe's confession, Paul D leaves 124 to stay in a church, pulling away from the community and focusing on his own past. Here he relives the disintegration of Sweet Home after Mr. Garner's death and reconsiders Mr. Garner's role in his suffering: "Now, plagued by the contents of his tobacco tin, he wondered how much difference there really was between before schoolteacher and after." He realizes now that he and his slave brothers, except for Sixo, were "isolated in a wonderful lie."

Upon Schoolteacher's arrival, this lie is fully exposed. Paul D recalls the failed escape from Sweet Home, his humiliation and degradation, and the death of his brother Sixo, who was tied to a tree and burned, but not before laughing wildly and yelling out "Seven-O," meaning that his lover, the Thirty Mile Woman, was pregnant with his child. Further, Paul D recalls being captured by Schoolteacher and learning the "dollar value of his weight, his strength, his heart, his brain, his penis, and his future." Slaves were not viewed as men or women, but as property, and Schoolteacher proves this belief by tracking down Sethe, who is worth more to him financially because she can "breed." Paul D's "rememory" ends with him in shackles with a bit in his mouth, and Mister, the rooster, having more freedom than he can even imagine.

In **chapter xxv**, Stamp Paid approaches Paul D who is alone and drinking on the steps of the church. Stamp Paid apologizes for showing him the newspaper clipping and offers Paul D lodging with anyone among the black community. Paul D assures him that Reverend Pike has already made such an offer, but that he prefers to be alone.

Stamp shares with Paul D the story of why he decided to change his name. While Stamp was a slave, his master's son took Stamp's wife as a concubine, raping her night after night, and Stamp could do nothing to stop it. This memory evokes Paul D's own questions about manhood and masculinity, and the "story becomes a ritual of affirmation for Stamp Paid and a rite of passage for Paul D." (Harris, 332) For Stamp Paid, the only way to move forward was to actually change his identity. In Sethe's defense, Stamp Paid tells Paul D what he saw the day Sethe killed her daughter, declaring, "She ain't crazy. She love those children. She was trying to outhurt the hurter." Part Two concludes with Paul D's reverberating, painful question, the question for himself and for America, "Tell me this one thing. How much is a nigger supposed to take? Tell me? How much?"

In Part Three, the bond between Sethe and Beloved tightens, and their raw emotions escalate as the relationship reveals its destructive quality. Sethe notices Beloved's neck scar, and, from then on, "the two of them cut Denver out of the games: the cooking games, the sewing games, the hair and dressing-up games. Games her mother loved so well she took to going to work later and later each day...." Sethe becomes obsessive about playing with Beloved, and she stops going to work altogether and eventually loses her job.

The play and games soon change into fighting. Beloved, tyrannical, takes "the best of everything," and she grows bigger and bigger, as if consuming Sethe. "She imitated Sethe, talked the way she did, laughed her laugh and used her body the same way down to the walk, the way Sethe moved her hands, sighed through her nose, held her head ... it was difficult for Denver to tell who was who." Figuratively, the past is now swallowing Sethe. She recounts, over and over, the painful stories Beloved craves, "and the more she took, the more Sethe began to talk, explain, describe how much she had suffered, been through, for her children." However, raging and furious, Beloved refuses to forgive Sethe for her past actions.

Denver realizes her job has changed from "protecting Beloved from Sethe ... to protecting her mother from Beloved." Neither Sethe nor Beloved seem concerned that the house is empty of food, and so finally Denver makes the crucial decision "to step off the edge of the world." She hesitates on the front porch, terrified to leave the premises of 124, and then she hears Baby Suggs's gentle laugh. Baby Suggs encourages her to go on, reminding her of her ancestors' courage and strength, including Sethe's.

The novel began with Denver crying because of the isolation and loneliness of 124; now she steps into the public eye, growing stronger as she enters the community. She first approaches Lady Jones, her old school teacher. When she tells Lady Jones that her mother is sick, Lady Jones calls her "baby," and "it was the word 'baby,' said softly and with such kindness, that inaugurated her life in the world as a woman." Denver helps to revive the role of the community. The women who have isolated Sethe for eighteen years now make up for this silence by providing for the family. Two days after Denver speaks with Lady Jones, she finds a sack of white beans lying on the tree stump at the edge of the yard. Each day there is something new, and these gifts force Denver to interact, as she must return the plates and bowls to the women in the neighborhood.

However, as "Denver's outside life improved, her home life deteriorated." Now re-energized with food, Sethe and Beloved resume their destructive relationship. Sometimes Beloved chokes at her own throat, drawing blood, and metaphorically swallowing Sethe: "The bigger Beloved got, the smaller Sethe became; the brighter Beloved's eyes, the more those eyes that used never to look away became slits of sleeplessness." Sethe fades as Beloved attempts to consume her, and Denver understands their cycle will never end: "Sethe was trying to make up for the handsaw; Beloved was making her pay for it." Sethe wants Beloved to understand why she cut her throat, that whites not only have the power to destroy you physically, but they can "dirty you." Sethe grapples with her past, facing her own guilt in the violent murder of her daughter.

Over the course of the novel, Denver transforms from an isolated and sheltered girl into the outgoing heroine of the novel. She takes responsibility for herself and her family: "It was a new thought, having a self to look out for and preserve." Denver seems to best understand the words Baby Suggs had been preaching, that her life is her own. She sets out for work, approaching the abolitionist couple, the Bodwins. When she tells their servant, Janey Wagon, about her mother and Beloved, Janey assumes Beloved is a ghost: "She got any lines in her hands?"

When Ella hears the story of how Beloved is slowly sucking the life out of Sethe, she organizes a rescue. Even though Ella had ostracized Sethe to punish Sethe for killing her own daughter, she, as an ex-slave, understands Sethe's motive. Ella's adolescence was spent as a sex slave, "shared by father and son," whom she considers "the lowest yet." Having been impregnated by her masters, she refused to nurse the baby, and after five days it died. This defiant act of refusing to nurse the rapist's baby symbolizes another act of a slave woman resisting her role as a subservient sexual object or "mammy." Ella believes the terrible past of slavery must not be allowed to reclaim its victims. She considers the ghost of the baby "an invasion" of the dead into the living, or the past into the present.

While Denver waits on the front porch for Mr. Bodwin to pick her up for her first day of work, the neighborhood women arrive at 124 with charms and religious objects. When they step up to 124, they envision younger versions of themselves: "The first thing they saw was not Denver sitting on the steps, but themselves. Younger, stronger, even as little girls lying in the grass asleep." These visions and memories evoke a sense of innocence and freedom, a form of "rememory" in which "positive moments instead of the painful oppressive past" give them strength. (Bowers, 223) The women pray, then sing, and the strength of the communal voices calls Sethe and Beloved to the doorway.

This climactic scene revolves around themes such as Sethe's relationship to community and the relationship of past and present. When Sethe hears the combined voices of the women, it is "as though the Clearing had come to her with all its heat and simmering leaves, where the voices of women searched for the right combination, the key, the code, the sound that broke the back of words ... It broke over Sethe and she trembled like the baptized in its wash." The image of the Clearing emphasizes the healing power of women come together, and the reference to baptism signifies that the moment will give Sethe a new beginning.

The women's voices, representing a version of call and response, finally save Sethe from being devoured by the past. Critics have stressed the role of the community in this scene, and its importance throughout the novel. "The power of the women's voices joined together has a creative capacity that symbolizes and ritualizes Sethe's cycle from spiritual death to rebirth" (Krumholz, 402), Linda Krumholz states. For Bouson, the women are "enacting a rescue fantasy and illustrating the potentially healing communality." (Bouson, 157) Bernard W. Bell cites how the scene evokes themes of "black kinship, motherhood, sisterhood, and love." (Bell, 10) Finally, Susan Bowers reminds us of Denver's role in the revival of this community: "Her efforts lead to everyone's salvation: the reunion of the community." (Bowers, 222)

The women act as a force against what they consider to be evil, the "devil-child." Yet the image that emerges of Beloved standing there naked and pregnant, "thunderblack and glistening," also evokes the image of a beautiful African ancestral mother. (Krumholz, 401) The pregnant Beloved symbolizes the true bridge between past and future. When Mr. Bodwin rides up, the "little hummingbirds" return to Sethe, and the scene suggests that she confuses Bodwin with Schoolteacher. But this time instead of killing herself or her child, she rushes after Bodwin. In this moment Beloved believes that Sethe is abandoning her as she stands alone on the porch, that the man without skin and a whip in hand "is looking at her," and in fear she runs away. It is Denver who stops her mother from attacking Bodwin and thus stops the cycle of the past overpowering the present. Corey argues that Denver "provides a link to the white community and a sign of potential interracial healing." (Corey, 45) Unlike Beloved, Denver can learn; she changes by the end. She has set in motion a maturation that will eventually make her an empowering ancestral spirit like Baby Suggs.

"Now 124 is quiet," **chapter xxvii** begins. Beloved is gone, although she is spotted by a stream, "cutting through the woods, a naked women with fish for hair," an image that refers to the African water spirit. (Corey, 37) Denver, who now looks more like her father, takes care of her mother. Denver also begins working for the Bodwins and makes plans to attend school, as Mrs. Bodwin plans to "experiment on her" and send her to Oberlin. This reference evokes Schoolteacher's dangerous experiments, and Susan Corey claims this reference exemplifies the "ambiguity" of the ending. (Corey, 46) However, Linda Krumholz takes a brighter view, arguing that Denver is now in position to "usurp schoolteacher's position; she must take away from him the power to define African-Americans." (Krumholz, 405) Denver has changed from a wholly dependent child to an independent woman, and she is a character who is able to acknowledge the past yet also move forward: "Denver represents both the future and the past: Denver will be the new African-American woman teacher, and she is Morrison's precursor, the woman who has taken on the task of carrying the story though generations to our storyteller." (Krumholz, 403)

Toward the end of the novel, Paul D finds Sethe lying in Baby Suggs's bed, un-bathed and fading out of reality, and he believes that she is planning to die, that she has given up. He promises to take care of her, and looking at her he recognizes there are "too many things to feel about this woman." When he first heard about Sethe's past, Paul D withdrew from Sethe and the community. Now he returns to her, his wandering finally over, and his present thoughts suggest that he has confronted and come to peace with both his and Sethe's past. He sees Sethe fully and realizes that she never judged him, as he had judged her. Lawrence suggests that now Paul D's memories "[are] constructive rather than destructive, giving him the freedom, finally, to chose his own desire." (Lawrence, 243) He now responds to Sethe with love and talk of the future, telling her, "[W]e got more yesterday than anybody. We need some kind of tomorrow." As Bowers explains, "only when characters can recover the past do they begin to imagine a future." (Bowers, 211) Now Paul can "put his story next to hers."

Sethe believes she has lost her daughter once again, calling Beloved her "best thing," and Paul disagrees, telling her, "You your best thing, Sethe. You are." Sethe's last question, "Me? Me?" affirms Baby Suggs's words, that loving oneself leads to freedom.

While Beloved represents an unchangeable past, Sethe, Paul D, and Denver illustrate possibilities of the present and future, as they evolve from slaves into free men and women.

By **chapter xxviii**, Beloved is no longer a fleshly form. She has "broken up," like her earlier fears. She has become a part of the background, "disremembered and unaccounted for." Although the narrative implies the community has forgotten her, it also reveals that "occasionally, however, the rustle of a skirt hushes when they wake," or that "her footprints come and go, come and go," stirring up memories of Beloved and all she symbolizes. Thus, her presence does not completely disappear.

The refrain that this "is not a story to pass on" works ironically, as of course the story has been passed on and continues to haunt: "*Beloved* is a work that is *passed on*—told and retold in the vast and proliferating critical conversation that surrounds it." (Bouson, 161)

"Beloved remains in the background as a haunting presence who reminds the community of those 'Sixty million and more,' untold stories of slavery and the Middle Passage," Susan Corey states. (Corey, 47) As the novel closes with one word, "Beloved," Morrison seems to be challenging the reader not to forget the tragedy of slavery. The character of Beloved has already demonstrated the consequences of trying to forget the past. As Trudier Harris points out, the "price of human existence cannot be placated through escapism—not that of Sethe killing her child, or of Baby Suggs willing herself to death, or any other form." (Harris, 340) In order to truly be free, the characters have finally faced the past, in all its horrors and degradations, and have found a way to live with its presence, while embracing their futures.

Works Cited

Barnett, Pamela E. "Figurations of Rape and the Supernatural in *Beloved*." *PMLA* 112, no. 3 (May 1997): 418–427.

Bell, Bernard W. "*Beloved*: A Womanist Neo-Slave Narrative; or Multivocal Remembrances of Things Past." *African American Review* 26, no. 1 (Spring 1992): 7–15.

Bouson, J. Brooks. " 'Whites Might Dirty Her All Right, but Not Her Best Thing,' The Dirtied and Traumatized Self of Slavery in *Beloved*." *Quiet As It's Kept: Shame, Trauma, and Race in the Novels of Toni Morrison*. Albany: State University of New York Press, 2000: 131–162.

Bowers, Susan. "*Beloved* and the New Apocalypse." *Toni Morrison's Fiction: Contemporary Criticism*. David L. Middleton, ed. New York: Garland Publishing, Inc., 2000: 213.

Corey, Susan. "Toward the Limits of Mystery: The Grotesque in Toni Morrison's *Beloved*," *The Aesthetics of Toni Morrison: Speaking the Unspeakable*. Marc C. Conner, ed. Jackson: University Press of Mississippi, 2000: 31–48.

Harris, Trudier. "Escaping Slavery but Not Its Images." *Toni Morrison:*

Critical Perspectives Past and Present. Henry Louis Gates, Jr., and K.A. Appiah, eds. New York: Amistad Press, 1993: 330–341.

Holloway, Karla. "*Beloved*: A Spiritual." *Callaloo* 13, no. 3 (1990): 516–525.

House, Elizabeth B. "Toni Morrison's Ghost: The Beloved Who is Not Beloved." *Studies in American Fiction* 18, no. 1 (Spring 1990): 17–26.

Jesser, Nancy. "Violence, Home, and Community in Toni Morrison's *Beloved.*" *African American Review* 33, no. 2 (Summer 1999): 332.

Krumholz, Linda. "The Ghosts of Slavery: Historical Recovery in Toni Morrison's *Beloved.*" *African American Review* 26, no. 2 (Autumn 1992): 395–408.

Lawrence, David. "Fleshly Ghosts and Ghostly Flesh: The Word and The Body in *Beloved.*" *Toni Morrison's Fiction: Contemporary Criticism*, David L. Middleton, ed. New York: Garland Publishing, Inc., 2000: 231–246.

Mobley, Marilyn Sanders. "A Different Remembering: Memory, History, and Meaning in *Beloved.*" *Toni Morrison: Critical Perspectives Past and Present.* Henry Louis Gates, Jr. and K.A. Appiah, eds. New York: Amistad Press, 1993: 356–365.

Smith, Valerie. "'Circling the Subject': History and Narrative in *Beloved.*" *Toni Morrison: Critical Perspectives Past and Present.* Henry Louis Gates, Jr. and K.A. Appiah, eds. New York: Amistad, 1993: 342–355.

Critical Views

KARLA F. C. HOLLOWAY ON SPIRITUALITY

Myth dominates the text. Not only has Morrison's reclamation of this story from the scores of people who interviewed Margaret Garner shortly after she killed her child in 1855 constituted an act of recovery, it has accomplished a mythic revisioning as well. Morrison refused to do any further research on Margaret Garner beyond her reviewing of the magazine article that recounted the astonishment of the preachers and journalists who found her to be "very calm ... very serene" after murdering her child (Rothstein). The imagination that restructures the initial article Morrison read into her novel *Beloved* is the imagination of a myth-maker. The mythological dimensions of her story, those that recall her earlier texts, that rediscover the altered universe of the black diaspora, that challenge the Western valuations of time and event (place and space) are those that, in various quantities in other black women writers and in sustained quantities in Morrison's works, allow a critical theory of text to emerge.[1]

Morrison revisions a history both spoken and written, felt and submerged. It is in the coalescence of the known and unknown elements of slavery—the events, minuscule in significance to the captors but major disruptions of black folks' experience in nurturing and loving and *being*—where Morrison's reconstruction of the historical text of slavery occurs. Morrison's reformulation propels a backlog of memories headlong into a postemancipation community that has been nearly spiritually incapacitated by the trauma of slavery. For Morrison's novel, what complicates the physical and psychic anguish is the reality that slavery itself *defies* traditional historiography. The victim's own chronicles of these events were systematically submerged, ignored, mistrusted, or superseded by "historians" of the era. This novel positions the consequences of black invisibility in both the records of slavery and the record-keeping as a situation of primary spiritual significance. Thus, the "ghostly"/"historical" presence that intrudes itself into this novel serves to belie the reportage that passes for historical records of this era as well as to reconstruct those lives into the spiritual ways that constituted the dimensions of their living. (...)

The structures within African and African-American novels consistently defy the collected eventualities of time "past, present, and future" and in consequence a consideration of aspect may be a more appropriate frame through which to consider the chronicle of events in this story.[7] Temporal time represents a narrow specific moment of occurrence. The relatively limited idea of time as being either in the past, the present, or the future is inadequate for a text like *Beloved*, where the pattern of events crisscrosses through these dimensions and enlarges the spaces that they suggest. This novel immediately makes it clear that a traditional (Western) valuation of time is not definitive of the experience it (re)members, instead it is an intrusion on a universe that has existed seemingly without its mediation. Weeks, months, and years become irrelevant to the spite of 124—the house that Beloved's spirit inhabits. Baby Suggs, Morrison writes, was "suspended between the nastiness of life and the meanness of the dead" (3–4). This suspension was shared by more than Baby Suggs. Living itself is suspended in this story because of the simultaneous presence of the past.

If Beloved is not only Sethe's dead daughter returned, but the return of all the faces, all the drowned, but remembered, faces of mothers and their children who have lost their being because of the force of that EuroAmerican slave-history, then she has become a cultural mooring place, a moment for reclamation and for naming. Morrison's epigraph to her novel cites the Old Testament: "I will call her Beloved who was not Beloved." I will call. I will name her who was not named. "I need to find a place to be," Beloved's discourse insists. Her being depended on not losing her self again. "Say my name," Beloved insists to Paul 17. She demands to be removed from her nothing-ness, to be specified, to be "called." (...)

If history has disabled human potential, then assertion, the ghostly insistence that Rich writes of in "Toward the Solstice" must come outside of history. Beloved's existence is liminal. Between worlds, being neither "in," nor "of" a past or a present, she is a confrontation of a killing history and a disabling present. Since neither aspect allows the kind of life that a postemancipation black community would have imagined for itself because at the very least, "not a house in the county ain't packed to the rafters with some dead Negro's grief" (5), *Beloved* becomes a text collected with the textures of living and dying rather than with a linear movements of events. Morrison has written novels marked by seasons (*The Bluest Eye*) and years (*Sula*) but this story is marked by the shifting presence of the house, number 124 on Bluestone Road, that was introduced in Book One as "spite[ful]," in Book Two as "loud," and in Book Three, as finally "quiet." This shift allows the focus of the novel to ignore the possible time frames. Neither distance nor years mattered to the white house where Beloved insisted herself back into reality. For Sethe, "the future was a matter of keeping the past at bay" (42) and since this story (not a story to "pass on") demystifies time, allowing it to "be" where/ whenever it must be, we know, even before the story assumes this "text," that there was neither future nor present in the woman who walked fully dressed out of the water.

The recursion of this text, its sublimation of time and its privileging of an alternative not only to history, but to reality, places it into the tradition of literature by black women because of its dependence on the alternative, the inversion that sustains the "place" that has replaced reality.[10] Certainly not all recursive texts sublimate time, but temporal displacement is clearly a possibility of such technique. This is why Hurston's note that black folk think in glyphs rather than writing is not only an acknowledgement of another cosmology, but an acknowledgement of the necessity of evolution in the basic design of the ways we think about thought. Thomas Kuhn's discussion in *The Structure of Scientific Revolutions* considers "evolution from the community's state of knowledge at any given time" (171) as the appropriate visual dimension of progress. It is evolution, i.e. a changing and shifting conceptualization that identifies the aspective nature of recursion, rather than temporicity as the operative narrative space of Morrison's text. In her re-visioning of the history of slavery, Morrison proposes a paradigm of that history that privileges the vision of its victims and that denies the closure of death as a way of side-stepping any of that tragedy. The houses of the counties held grief; Sethe practiced, without success, holding back the past, and Beloved held not only her own history, but those of "sixty million and more." In these ways, the vision of this novel is innervision, the cognitive reclamation of our spiritual histories.

Notes

1. My position is that a critical theory of black *women's* writing emerges as the dimensions of a cultural expression within an African-American literary tradition and specifies, through an interpretation of literary style and substance and its formal modes and figurations, certain textual modes of discourse. Such a specification underscores my primary argument that black women's literature reflects its community—its cultural ways of knowing as well as its ways of framing that knowledge in language. The figures of language that testify to that cultural mooring place—the inversive, recursive, and sometimes even subversive structures that layer the black text—give it a dimension only accessed when the cultural and gendered points of its initiation are acknowledged.

7. Aspect describes action in terms of its duration without a consideration of its place in time. In *Caribbean and African Languages* Morgan Dalphinis's discussion explores how aspect is a better descriptor of such basic cultural concepts than those traditionally measured by a "(past/present/future) time-based yardstick" (87). The implications of such a measure for literature that reflects its culture in the arrangement and use of language is clearly relevant to literatures of the African diaspora.

10. Black literary theory's interest in the nature of inversion in the black text provides some rich critical discussion and speculation. Houston Baker has provided one of the most interesting comments on this strategy. He writes, in *Blues, Ideology, and Afro-American Literature*, that "mythic and literary acts of language are not intended or designed for communicative ends. Rather than informational or

communicative utterances that assure harmonious normalcy in human cultures such linguistic acts are radically contingent events whose various readings or performances occasion *inversive* symbolic modes of cognition and other extra-ordinary human responses" (my emphasis, 122). Baker's comment formulates a particularly important rubric for the discussion in this essay. The dissolution of "normalcy" would seem to predicate the "inversive" cognitive and narrative strategies in *Beloved*. However, the importance of inversion signaling subversion in black women's writing is the dimension that is distinct to a feminist canon. In *The Signifying Monkey*, Gates identifies the "mystery type of narrative discourse" as one "characterized by plot inversions." These, he notes, function "of course" as temporal inversions." His point is to illustrate Ishmael Reed's texts as a "sort of indeterminacy" that predicates the use of inversion as textual "impediment." Impediment is somewhat closer to the subversion I describe, but it implies a blockage that is not a feature of the black woman writer's use of this technique.

BERNARD W. BELL:
A SOCIOPSYCHOLOGICAL VIEW

On a sociopsychological level, *Beloved* is the story of Sethe Suggs's quest for social freedom and psychological wholeness. Sethe struggles with the haunting memory of her slave past and the retribution of Beloved, the ghost of the infant daughter that she killed in order to save her from the living death of slavery. On a legendary and mythic level, *Beloved* is a ghost story that frames embedded narratives of the impact of slavery, racism, and sexism on the capacity for love, faith, and community of black families, especially of black women, during the Reconstruction period. Set in post-Civil-War Cincinnati, *Beloved* is a womanist neo-slave narrative of double consciousness, a postmodern romance that speaks in many compelling voices and on several time levels of the historical rape of black American women and of the resilient spirit of blacks in surviving as a people.

As the author has explained in interviews and as a sympathetic white minister's report in the February 12, 1856, issue of the *American* Baptist reveals (see Bassett), at the center of *Beloved* is Morrison's retelling of the chilling historical account of a compassionate yet resolute self-emancipated mother's tough love. Margaret Garner, with the tacit sympathy of her sexagenarian mother-in-law, cut the throat of one of her four children and tried to kill the others to save them from the outrages of slavery that she had suffered. Guided by the spirits of the many thousands gone, as inscribed in her dedication, Morrison employs a multivocal text and a highly figurative language to probe her characters' double consciousness of their terribly paradoxical circumstances as people and non-people in a social arena of white male hegemony. She also foregrounds infanticide as a desperate act of "'thick'" love (164) by a fugitive-slave mother "with iron eyes and backbone to match" (9). "'Love is or it ain't,'" Sethe, the dramatized narrator/protagonist, says in reproach to a shocked friend, Paul D. "'Thin love ain't love at all'" (164). Indignantly reflecting on Paul D's metonymic reprimand that she "'got two feet ... not four'" (165), she later expands on their oppositional metaphors in reverie: "Too thick, he said. My love was too thick. What he know about it? Who in the world is he willing to die for? Would he give his privates to a stranger in return for a carving?" (203).

The implied author, the version of herself that Morrison creates as she creates the narrative (see Booth 70–75, 138, 151), brilliantly dramatizes the moral, sexual, and epistemological distances between Sethe and Paul D. After their first dialogue, a trackless, quiet forest abruptly appears between them. This metaphorical silence is an ingenious, ironic use of the technique of call and response that invites the implied reader—in Wolfgang Iser's words, that "network of response-inviting structures, which impel the reader to grasp the text" (34)—to pause and take stock of his or her own ambivalent moral and visceral responses to this slave mother's voicing of her thick love.

Thematically, the implied author interweaves racial and sexual consciousness in *Beloved*. Sethe's black awareness and rejection of white perceptions and inscriptions of herself, her children, and other slaves as nonhuman—marking them by letter, law, and lash as both animals and property—are synthesized with her black feminist sense of self-sufficiency. Sethe reconciles gender differences with first her husband Halle Suggs, and later Paul D, in heterosexual, endogamous relationships that affirm the natural and Biblical principles of the racial and ethnic survival of peoplehood through procreation and parenting in extended families. Although the implied author blends racial and sexual consciousness, the structure and style of the text foreground the ambivalence of slave women about motherhood that violates their personal integrity and that of their family.

Foregrounding the theme of motherhood, Morrison divides the text into twenty-eight unnumbered mini-sections, the usual number of days in a woman's monthly menstrual cycle, within three larger, disproportionate sections. Within these sections, Sethe experiences twenty-eight happy days of "having women friends, a mother-in-law, and all of her children together; of being part of a neighborhood; of, in fact, having neighbors at all to call her own" (173). Also within these sections, the passion and power of memory ebb and flow in a discontinuous, multivocal discourse of the present with the past. Unlike the univocal, nineteenth-century slave narratives, in which plot rides character in the protagonist's journey of transformation from object to subject, *Beloved* is a haunting story of a mother's love that frames a series of interrelated love stories (maternal, parental, filial, sororal, conjugal, heterosexual, familial, and communal) by multiple narrators. These stories begin in 1873 and end in 1874, but flash back intermittently to 1855. In the flashbacks and reveries, the omniscient narrator invokes ancestral black women's remembrances of the terror and horror of the Middle Passage. She also probes the deep physical and psychic wounds of Southern slavery, especially the paradoxes and perversities of life on Sweet Home plantation in Kentucky, and recalls Sethe's bold flight to freedom in Ohio in 1855. Freedom, as Paul D's and Sethe's stories most dramatically illustrate, is "to get to a place where you could love anything you chose—not to need permission for desire" (162).

The metaphors of personal and communal wholeness in the text heighten the psychological realism of its womanist themes of black kinship, motherhood, sisterhood, and love. Besides the structural analogue to a woman's natural reproductive cycle, the text frequently and dramatically highlights metaphors and metonyms for the agony and ecstasy, despair and hope, of loving, birthing, nurturing, and bonding. Heart, breasts, milk, butter, water, and trees—these recurring tropes first appear in the opening eight mini-sections as the vehicles for controlling the psychological emotional, and moral distances among the narrators, characters, and implied reader, who participate, on various levels, in Sethe's historical and mythic quest.

After the omniscient narrator introduces us to the restless, spiteful spirit of Sethe's two-year-old daughter Beloved, we are quickly and irrevocably drawn into the vortex of conflicting values and feelings of the text. On one hand, we are drawn emotionally and psychologically closer to Sethe through her unrelenting memory of the terrible price she has paid for loving her daughter so dearly; but on the other, like Paul D and Ella, we are at first morally repelled by her gory act of infanticide. When slave catchers and schoolteacher suddenly appear in the family's Ohio yard to return Sethe and her children to slavery, she not only cuts Beloved's throat with a handsaw and attempts to kill her other three, but she subsequently trades ten minutes of sex on her daughter's grave with an engraver, as his son watches, to pay him for carving the word Beloved on her daughter's headstone.

Our sympathies for Sethe are strengthened, however, through her grim reverie and dialogue with Paul D. Through them we discover that, earlier in 1855, while pregnant with Denver and before she could escape with her husband Halle to join their children in Ohio with the milk to nurse her baby girl, she was outrageously violated. "I am full God damn it of two boys with mossy teeth," she remembers, "one sucking on my breast the other holding me down, their book-reading teacher watching and writing it up." Weaving into her story the additional gruesome details provided eighteen years later by Paul D, who knew her from their shared years of slavery on the ironically named Sweet Home plantation, the horror continues:

Add my husband to it, watching, above me in the loft—hiding close by—the one place he thought no one would look for him, looking down on what I couldn't look at at all. And not stopping them—looking and letting it happen ... There is also my husband squatting by the churn smearing the butter as well as its clabber all over his face because the milk they took is on his mind. And as far as he is concerned, the world may as well know it. (70)

Again we note the implied author's privileging of metaphor and metonym over black dialect to achieve just the right aesthetic balance between the poetics and polemics of the long black song of the many thousands gone that she skillfully orchestrates to engage our hearts and mind.

LINDA KRUMHOLZ ON RITUALS

Morrison uses ritual as a model for the healing process. Rituals function as formal events in which symbolic representations—such as dance, song, story, and other activities—are spiritually and communally endowed with the power to shape real relations in the world. In *Beloved*, ritual processes also imply particular notions of pedagogy and epistemology in which—by way of contrast with dominant Western traditions—knowledge is multiple, context-dependent, collectively asserted, and spiritually derived. Through her assertion of the transformative power of ritual and the incorporation of rituals of healing into her narrative, Morrison invests the novel with the potential to construct and transform individual consciousness as well as social relations.

To make the novel work as a ritual, Morrison adapts techniques from Modernist novels, such as the fragmentation of the plot and a shifting narrative voice, to compel the reader to actively construct an interpretive framework. In *Beloved* the reader's process of reconstructing the fragmented story parallels Sethe's psychological recovery: Repressed fragments of the (fictionalized) Personal and historical past are retrieved and reconstructed. Morrison also introduces oral narrative techniques—repetition, the blending of voices, a shifting narrative voice, and an episodic framework—that help to simulate the aural, participatory dynamics of ritual within the private, introspective form of the novel. In many oral traditions, storytelling and poetry are inseparable from ritual, since words as sounds are perceived as more than concepts; they are events with consequences. Morrison uses Modernist and oral techniques in conjunction with specifically African-American cultural referents, both historical and symbolic, to create a distinctly African-American voice and vision which, as in Baby Suggs's rituals, invoke the spiritual and imaginative power to teach and to heal.

The central ritual of healing—Sethe's "rememory" of and confrontation with her past—and the reader's ritual of healing correspond to the three sections of the novel. In part one the arrival first of Paul D then of Beloved forces Sethe to confront her past in her incompatible roles as a slave and as a mother. Moving from the fall of 1873 to the winter, the second part describes Sethe's period of atonement, during which she is enveloped by the past, isolated in her house with Beloved, who forces her to suffer over and over again all the pain and shame of the past. Finally, part three is Sethe's ritual "clearing," in which the women of the community aid her in casting out the voracious Beloved, and Sethe experiences a repetition of her scene of trauma with a difference—this time she aims her murderous hand at the white man who threatens her child.

The three phases of the reader's ritual also involve a personal reckoning with the history of slavery. In part one, stories of slavery are accumulated through fragmented recollections, culminating in the revelation of Sethe's murder of her child in the last chapters of the section. In part two, the reader is immersed in the voices of despair. Morrison presents the internal voices of Sethe, Denver, and Beloved in a ritual chant of possession, while Paul D and Stamp Paid are also overwhelmed by the legacy of slavery. The last part of the novel is the reader's "clearing," achieved through the comic relief of the conversation of Paul D and Stamp Paid and the hopeful reunion of Sethe and Paul D. The novel concludes with Denver's emergence as the new teacher, providing the reader with a model for a new pedagogy and the opportunity for the reconstruction of slave history from a black woman's perspective.

Finally, while *Beloved* can be read as a ritual of healing, there is also an element of disruption and unease in the novel, embodied in the character of Beloved. As an eruption of the past and the repressed unconscious, Beloved catalyzes the healing process for the characters and for the reader; thus, she is a disruption necessary for healing. But Beloved also acts as a trickster figure who defies narrative closure or categorization, foreclosing the possibility of a complete "clearing" for the reader. Thus, as the reader leaves the book, we have taken on slavery's haunt as our own.[4]

Note

4. Morrison writes, in her essay "Unspeakable Things Unspoken," that the purpose of this haunting of the reader "is to keep the reader preoccupied with the nature of the incredible spirit world while being supplied e controlled diet of the incredible political world" (32).

TRUDIER HARRIS ON IMAGES OF SLAVERY

Ownership and possession are characteristic of slavery. They reflect the monetary exchange involved in that system of dehumanization as well as the psychological control usually attendant upon the physical imprisonment. I am using "ownership" here to refer to the practice of masters having legal rights to the bodies and labor of their slaves. I am using "possession" to refer to the psychological dimension of the relationship, in which masters were able to convince some slaves to believe in the institution of slavery and to concede that their situation was hopeless. These mind-controlling tactics took a variety of forms, beginning with the destruction of family and linguistic groups in the assigning of slaves to plantations in the New World. The psychological damage attendant upon realizing that one was separated from blood relatives and kinspeople, essentially alone in the world, worked to the benefit of the slaveholder and was designed to teach dependency in the slave. At the least sign of uppityness, slaveholders could further "break" slaves with a series of barbaric punishments, including whipping, branding a letter on the face or back, cropping an ear or a finger, confining them in bits, or selling them "down the river," which had connotations of horror that far outstripped any actual physical punishment. All of these tactics were everyday reminders to slaves that the masters possessed their very minds and memories—had indeed erased if not destroyed their histories—even as they owned their bodies. (...)

With all of this offering up of sacrifices to human misery, with all these "gifts" having been extracted from the former slaves, it is somewhat surprising that one of the recurring images in the novel is debt-based, as if these characters, who were existentially if not nominally free during slavery, still have external claims upon their personhood, as if they still, inexplicably, have debts to pay. At striking jolts in the narrative, Morrison reverts our attention to the buying and selling of human beings by inserting images of monetary units to describe physical features and to convey states such as frustration and remorse. She suggests thereby that the characters are not as free as they now profess to be, that they have inadvertently inculcated concepts of value from their slave masters, frequently to their own detriment. She also uses the imagery ironically to comment on current practices or incidents in the black community that bring to mind those bartering notions of ownership from slavery, which suggest that *some* black people may have modeled their behavior too closely on that of their masters. And she textures the language with images of finance to remind readers constantly of the overall outline and subject of the novel: the unrelenting psychological and physical damage from a system where human beings were equated to poker chips.

Monetary images also become the language of desire in the novel, as characters express their greatest wants in financial terms. Denver recognizes Beloved long before Sethe does and believes that she is the long-lost Presence (like Pauline waiting for Cholly Breedlove) who will make a difference in her life. Denver does not want to question Beloved overly much for fear that she will leave. She therefore resigns herself to be content to gaze upon Beloved, to stare at her in a hunger-fulfilling strategy that savors Beloved's presence and stifles the urge to ask questions about how she came to be in 124 Bluestone Road: " ... she was careful to appear uninquisitive about the things she was dying to ask Beloved, for if she pressed too hard, she might lose the penny that the held-out palm wanted, and lose, therefore, the place beyond appetite." Denver's desire to keep Beloved is perhaps as great as Beloved's desire to stay and possess Sethe. The expression of both desires in a single, shiny penny points to the childishness in both girls, to the intensity with which they hope to achieve their objectives. The simplicity of the penny crystallizes desire as a part of the ownership-possession theme. The penny is basic, elemental, first on the scale of value; it therefore connotes that basic, unbridled desire is not to be denied.

While desire might seem simple, easily met, its depth is masked—by the use of the coin imagery as well as by the demeanor that Beloved initially presents. This simple country girl who seems to have lost her way and just stumbled into 124 Bluestone Road is really a sinister presence intent upon having her way at all costs. The value of the coin is inversely proportional to the intensity of Beloved's desire, just as value assigned to human beings during slavery was similarly mismatched, sometimes dangerously so—as in the case of the gap between Sixo's assumed value and his violent actions.

Morrison shows how the past continues to impinge upon the future by tying its possibilities to her monetary imagery. She refers to the "coin of life" when Paul D is trying to forge a future with Sethe after his indiscretion with Beloved. Paul D meets Sethe at the restaurant to tell her of his brief affair with Beloved, but he ends up asking her to have a baby with him.

The request is a stalling action at a crucial moment in their relationship; it could have dire consequences for their future, yet Paul D is willing to take the chance. "Still, he'd gotten a little more time, bought it, in fact, and hoped the price wouldn't wreck him. Like paying for an afternoon in the coin of life to come."[3] Since so much misery for these two in the past has depended upon the monetary value placed on them or their relatives, it is ironic that the same images, reinforced by repetition ("bought," "price," "paying," "coin"), would be used to describe their potential for post-slavery happiness. The threat to that potential makes their future just as precarious as the lives of Paul A, Paul F, and Sixo during slavery.

Paul D is gambling on his future in the way that Southern slaveholders used human ante in their games on the riverboats of the Mississippi, or the way that Baby Suggs's seducers/rapists/owners played checkers with her children and relatives. Is there too much of a tendency to possession in the relationship to put it on any other than a monetary footing? Have the very psyches of these former slaves been so saturated with the prices placed on them (Schoolteacher taught Paul D "the dollar value of his weight, his strength, his heart, his brain, his penis, and his future") that they cannot conceive of worth in any other way?

At another key juncture in the novel, Morrison also selects her comparative images from finance. Stamp feels that the memory of Baby Suggs is "scorching his soul like a silver dollar in a fool's pocket" when he contemplates the damage he may have done to the memory of their friendship by telling Paul D about Sethe killing Beloved. What Stamp has done could potentially destroy Sethe and ruin her chances for happiness with Paul D. It is appropriate that such an act weighs on his soul, especially since he has spent his life lifting burdens from black people's souls. Like the fool who is overeager to spend his fortune, Stamp becomes overly anxious to make up for his indiscretion in telling Paul D about Sethe. But the imagery also works in another way: the gap between the silver dollar and the fool's ability to estimate value is symbolically the gap between Stamp's intent and the outcome of his showing Paul D that destructive newspaper clipping about Sethe. It is also the gap between true human worth and the monetary value slaveholders would have assigned to such worth. Stamp has thus violated his own philosophy and erroneously assumed that there was yet another price Sethe had to pay for her place in the world, a price that may mean the end of her happiness. In that brief slip in his philosophy, Stamp also shares kinship with those slaveholders who would continue to extract pay, further "gifts," from people whose accounts should all be stamped "paid."

Stamp tries to mitigate this violation by approaching Sethe's house with a talisman of his debt-free philosophy. He carries a faded red ribbon from the head of a lynched (possibly raped) young black girl ("He clutched the red ribbon in his pocket for strength"); it reminds him of his gift of his wife to his master because Vashti had worn a black ribbon to all of her meetings with her seducer/owner (he had given it to her). Stamp "fingers" and "worries" the ribbon like a worn dollar bill; the debt he owns to Baby Suggs's memory gets wrapped up with the victimization of his wife and the young girl and the knowledge that their debtors did not pay, and with the debt he now owes Sethe for having threatened her future. The only account-balancing option he has is to pay off his debt to Sethe.

Although slavery is over, black people are still judging each other through the eyes and with the units of measure of those who enslaved them. For the brief moment when Stamp has told Paul D about Sethe, he has abandoned his usual generosity and has joined in sentiment with the black townspeople who have punished Baby Suggs for what they perceive as her uppityness by not warning her about the approaching schoolteacher (as the people in the Bottom avoid Sula for not adhering to their mores). They have concluded that she should pay for her pride in the same way that a slaveholder might conclude that an uppity slave should be punished. Judgment tied to value and expressed in coins ironically shows the human faults in black people that align them with their enslavers. The higher goal of freedom has not yet been complemented with a *consistent* higher goal of morality.

The coin imagery surfaces again when Denver finally gets enough nerve to leave 124 and ask neighbors for help. She encounters an image at the Bodwin house not unlike the Sambo doll that haunts the Invisible Man:

> ... she had seen, sitting on a shelf by the back door, a blackboy's mouth full of money. His head was thrown back farther than a head could go, his hands were shoved in his pockets. Bulging like moons, two eyes were all the face he had above the gaping red mouth. His hair was a cluster of raised, widely spaced dots made of nail heads. And he was on his knees. His mouth, wide as a cup, held the coins needed to pay for a delivery or some other small service, but could just as well have held buttons, pins or crab-apple jelly. Painted across the pedestal he knelt on were the words "At Yo Service."

This object is quickly recognizable as one of the many images of Sambo, as Joseph Boskin makes clear in *Sambo: The Rise and Demise of an American Jester* (New York: Oxford, 1986) and as the film, *Ethnic Notions*, traces through an extensive period of American history. Sambo is the image of black people controlled by white people, usually signalled by its distorted facial features, especially eyes and mouth, and its exuding of a palpable willingness to please. In history as in literature, Sambo is ever self-effacing, ever obsequious and subservient, ever willing "to grin and bear it," ever willing to be trampled on by whites because its irrepressible spirit will rise up and beg to be degraded again. This popular stereotype of black people saturated the white American mind for centuries; not only was it complimentary to whites, whose money could evoke such distorted grins, but it was comforting to them, for it was infinitely more pleasant to imagine grinning darkies than knife-wielding ones.

It is ironic that this stereotypical image is in the home of the Bodwins, who were formerly abolitionists, yet it makes clear how pervasive the Sambo stereotype was, how even so-called liberals could not resist its "charm." This minstrel Sambo alludes as well to the gift-giving nature that has been identified with blacks throughout the novel. Slaves by their nature are presumed to exist for the service of their masters. In addition to his regular services as a slave, Halle has served Garner with five years of Sundays in exchange for Baby Suggs (who has paused in the Bodwin kitchen with Janey), and Sethe and the Sweet Home men could document a volume of services they have rendered without remuneration. As a female slave, Baby Suggs has had the additional responsibility of servicing her masters sexually, just as Nan has been forced to nurture their offspring at her breasts. Whether as mammies or sluts, or sometimes sexual partners, or cooks, or nursemaids, black women were especially in the service of their masters during slavery. One dominant image Sethe has retained of herself from that period is that of someone who has "enough for all," whether it is milk for Beloved and Denver, meat for the dogs at Sawyer's Restaurant, or food and milk for Paul D, Denver, and Beloved; she has always been at somebody's service, whether voluntarily or not.

It is noteworthy that this Sambo caricature could have had other functions, just as black people could have been defined (and some did define themselves) in healthier ways during slavery. But it is Denver who observes and imprints the image on her mind. What is its significance to her? While it would be questionable to say that she is astute enough to understand the complex psychological warping and role confinement that slavery produced, she has nonetheless heard and seen some of the consequences in her own family. She had expected to escape such degradation of the human spirit by going to the Bodwins to ask for work. If they have such an image in their home, perhaps it serves as a forewarning to her of what she can become and must guard against. Service need not mean distortion of the human spirit. With this image before her, perhaps Denver is being offered a choice for how to shape her own destiny: give good work in exchange for pay but remember that even *good* white folks may create situations that could be benignly destructive to black people not on guard against such a possibility (former abolitionists need not necessarily support social equality). Without a modicum of that level of analysis, however, Denver can simply note that the Sambo object is black and distorted, but that it is grotesquely happy to be giving. If she merely concludes that it is not what she wants to be, her pausing to observe the Sambo would have served its purpose, would have suggested an alternative pattern of behavior in interacting with whites.

Though the repulsive object is not immediately tied to Sethe and Beloved, it is nonetheless against the backdrop of their interactions that Denver has a chance to observe it. It therefore keeps the notion of value before us and prompts, at this position in the story, our consideration of whether or not Sethe has become the wide-eyed, gaping servant willing to suffer any humiliation at Beloved's hands. Are her actions with Beloved mirrored in the subservience of the object Denver sees? Has Sethe, in spite of fighting so valiantly to escape from slavery, allowed her own value to slip until she becomes the "nigger-slave" to Beloved's "masterful," authoritative presence? The coinage of exchange, the dynamics of value have now come to undermine the mother/daughter relationship that Sethe sought so desperately to release from the system of bartering with human lives.

Like an insatiable, exacting slave master who feels entitled to service, Beloved never gets enough of anything; all of Sethe's efforts must be exerted for her pleasure.

Anything she wanted she got, and when Sethe ran out of things to give her, Beloved invented desire.... She took the best of everything—first. The best chair, the biggest piece, the prettiest plate, the brightest ribbon for her hair ... When once or twice Sethe tried to assert herself—be the unquestioned mother whose word was law and who knew what was best—Beloved slammed things, wiped the table clean of plates, threw salt on the floor, broke a windowpane.

Beloved's power resides in Sethe's willingness to please; though it is based in guilt, its surface manifestation is no different from that of the acquiescent slave who believes that, other possibilities notwithstanding, his destiny resides with his master, and he is just as willing to serve as the stereotypical Sambo suggests. Sethe, too, has learned this relationship in slavery even if she has not previously been called upon to display that knowledge.

This objectification of the relationship between Sethe and Beloved clarifies for Denver toward whom her sympathies should be directed. Though she may have wished fervently for Beloved's presence, any power strong enough to reduce her mother to such obsequiousness does not need further assistance from her. For as certainly as the object is cast in its kneeling and serving position, just as certainly something or someone has conceptualized it as such and reduced it to that status. Indeed, it is appropriate in this analysis that the creator of the object is not visible, for it ties in nicely with Beloved's questionable origins and make-up. The Sambo, then, further serves to strengthen Denver's realization that she is the only member of the trio detached enough from the situation to do anything about it.

The theme of payment connected to the Sambo harks back to an earlier observation Denver has made of what she owes for the difficulty of her birth. She especially savors the story when she is relating it to Beloved.

> Denver stopped and sighed. This was the part of the story she loved. She was coming to it now, and she loved it because it was all about herself; but she hated it too because it made her feel like a bill was owing somewhere and she, Denver, had to pay it. But who she owed or what to pay it with eluded her.

Unconsciously, Denver has adopted the measures she has heard her mother use to define relationships during slavery; even as Sethe holds the crying Denver in her arms shortly after Paul D's arrival, she asserts: "No more running—from nothing. I will never run from another thing on this earth. I took one journey and I paid for the ticket, but let me tell you something,

Paul D Garner: it cost too much! Do you hear me? It cost too much." Certainly we can tie references to the cost of human bodies to the usual colloquial expressions of benefit received to energy exerted, but the images nonetheless, in this context, also connect the value relationships directly to those from which the characters have recently escaped. By venturing out to ask help from the neighbors, Denver is "buying her mother's freedom," releasing her from slavery, in ways comparable to those in which Halle "paid for" Baby Suggs; Denver is offering up her labor, her "gift" to misery, just as her father has done earlier.

In describing physical features, Morrison uses the nickel as her monetary frame of reference. At Lady Jones's house on her first solo outing in many years, Denver reveals such innocence that Lady Jones perceives her eyes as "nickel-round," reflective of the child-like state in which the sheltered Denver has remained. Connotations of the wide-eyed, frightened slave and the buck-eyed minstrel also come to mind, for eyes have been one of the central focal points of stereotyping black people throughout their history in America (as they—and the mouth—are in the image in the Bodwin kitchen). Denver has attended Lady Jones' school briefly with "a beautiful boy as smart as she was with a birthmark like a nickel on his cheek." The latter image almost literally evokes the notion of branding slaves; the suggestion of a coin undermines these symbolic acts of value and ownership and goes directly to the foundation of the system: economics.

Ultimately, these monetary images succeed in sending mixed messages about how well the characters in *Beloved* have succeeded in transcending slavery. If black people are indeed free of slavery, then why burden them with evocations of that condition?[4] If they indeed have a superior morality (as Stamp Paid implies when he observes about white people—"What *are* these people?" and as Baby Suggs implies when she asserts "There is no bad luck in the world but whitefolks"), then why is it so confused? But perhaps that is precisely the point. Perhaps Morrison once again makes clear the futility of trying to find any absolutes in such a distorted, complex world. I would maintain, however, that it is necessary to have some stable point of reference—even when values are not absolute. There must be something to balance the horror of slavery; otherwise, why would slaves risk so much to be free? If the coinage imagery sends mixed messages, then perhaps Morrison's overall message about slavery and black people's transcendence of it is itself ambivalent.

Or perhaps she is redirecting the imagery to comment on the distorted relationships that exist in the novel. The possession theme usually associated with slavery is certainly relevant in a discussion of the interactions of Sethe, Beloved, and Denver. All of the women emphasize possession-ownership over love. Denver asserts her claim to Beloved after Beloved almost chokes Sethe to death in Baby Suggs's Clearing: "Whatever her power and however she used it, Beloved was *hers.* Sethe asserts her claim to her children by gathering them all together in an effort to save them from Schoolteacher. Beloved asserts her claim to Sethe by virtue of having been killed. And they all assert their claims to each other in the litany of passages that reverberate with ownership.

Is ownership, ostensibly with love as its basis, any different from ownership by designation as chattel? Or are these women locked in a duel that is potentially more destructive than slavery? Sethe has exhibited almost superhuman qualities in escaping from slavery in her pregnant condition. She has also shown uncommon self-possession during slavery, when she witnessed the lynching of her mother, the lynching of Paul F, and numerous other atrocities. None of these incidents has brought on insanity. Yet she borders on that state under Beloved's demands. She has remained a functional human being through all her trials and tribulations, yet she becomes dysfunctional upon Beloved's arrival. Is her love, as Paul D asserts, "too thick"? Can Sethe's and Beloved's perceptions of mother love or sister love, as they are manifested here, be put on the same par of anathema with slavery? In carving out a definition of motherhood in a world where she had no models for that status, in shaping a concept of love from a void, Sethe has erred on the side of excess, a destructive excess that inadvertently gives primacy to the past and death rather than to life and the future.

How can these women so locked in the past find a road to the future? The ownership-subservience tied to the coinage imagery occurs at important decision-making points in the novel, where characters have the option of moving forward to the future or returning to the past. All of these points presumably occur where human interaction is voluntary rather than forced, yet the characters frequently continue the forced interactions of previous conditions. Thus the question becomes one of how to confront the past, make one's peace with it, and move on into the future.

Notes

3. Later in this scene, Sethe and Paul D walk through a snowstorm where the flakes are "fat enough and heavy enough to crash like nickels on stone."

4. Certainly the novel is about reconciling oneself to the past, but the haunting in these sometimes seemingly innocuous ways raises more issues than it resolves.

PAMELA E. BARNETT ON RAPE
AND THE SUPERNATURAL

Toni morrison's *Beloved* is haunted by history, memory, and a specter that embodies both; yet it would be accurate to say that *Beloved* is haunted by the history and memory of rape specifically. While Morrison depicts myriad abuses of slavery like brutal beatings and lynchings, the depictions of and allusions to rape are of primary importance; each in some way helps explain the infanticide that marks the beginnings of Sethe's story as a free woman.[1] Sethe kills her child so that no white man will ever "dirty" her, so that no young man with "mossy teeth" will ever hold the child down and suck her breasts (251, 70). Of all the memories that haunt Morrison's characters, those that involve sexual abuse and exploitation hold particular power: rape is the trauma that forces Paul D to lock his many painful memories in a "tobacco tin" heart (113), that Sethe remembers more vividly than the beating that leaves a tree of scars on her back, that destroys Halle's mind. and against which Ella measures all evil.

I say that the book is haunted by rape not to pun idly on the ghostly presence that names the book but to establish the link between haunting and rape that invigorates the novel's dominant trope: the succubus figure.[2] The character Beloved is not just the host of Sethe's dead child: she is a succubus, a female demon and nightmare figure that sexually assaults male sleepers and drains them of semen.[3] The succubus figure, which is related to the vampire, another sexualized figure that drains a vital fluid, was incorporated into African American folklore in the form of shape-shifting witches who "ride" their terrified victims in the night (Puckett 568),[4] and Beloved embodies the qualities of that figure as well. In separate assaults, Beloved drains Paul D of semen and Sethe of vitality: symptomatically, Beloved's body swells as she also feeds off her victims' horrible memories of and recurring nightmares about sexual violations that occurred in their enslaved past. But Beloved functions as more than the receptacle of remembered stories; she reenacts sexual violation and thus figures the persistent nightmares common to survivors of trauma.[5] Her insistent manifestation constitutes a challenge for the characters who have survived rapes inflicted while they were enslaved: directly and finally communally, to confront a past they cannot forget. Indeed, it is apparent forgetting that subjects them to traumatic return: confrontation requires a direct attempt at remembering.

Morrison uses the succubus figure to represent the effects of institutionalized rape under slavery. When the enslaved persons' bodies were violated, their reproductive potential was commodified. The succubus, who rapes and steals semen, is metaphorically linked to such rapes and to the exploitation of African Americans' reproduction. Just as rape was used to dehumanize enslaved persons, the succubus' or vampire's assault robs victims of vitality, both physical and psychological. By representing a female rapist figure and a male rape victim,

Morrison foregrounds race, rather than gender; its the category determining domination or subjection to rape.

History and Collective Memory: "The Serious Work of Beating Back the Past"

Two memories of rape that figure prominently in the novel echo the succubus's particular form of sexual assault. The narrator refers several times to the incident in which two "mossy-toothed" boys (70) hold Sethe down and suck her breast milk (6, 16–17, 31, 68–70, 200, 228). No less important, Paul D works on a chain gang in Alfred, Georgia, where prisoners are forced to fellate white guards every morning (107–09, 229). In addition, Ella is locked up and repeatedly raped by a father and son she calls "the lowest yet" (119, 256), and Stamp Paid's wife, Vashti, is forced into sex by her enslaver (184, 232). Baby Suggs is compelled to have sex with a straw boss who later breaks his coercive promise not to sell her child (23) and again with an overseer (144). Sethe's mother is "taken up many times by the crew" during the Middle Passage (62), as are many other enslaved women (180). And three women in the novel—Sethe's mother, Baby Suggs, and Ella—refuse to nurse babies conceived through rape. Other allusions to sexual violation include the Sweet Home men's dreams of rape (10, 11), Sethe's explanation for adopting the mysterious Beloved— her fears that white men will "jump on" a homeless, wandering black girl (68)—and the neighborhood suspicion that Beloved is the black girl rumored to have been imprisoned and sexually enslaved by a local white man who has recently died (119, 235). There are also acts of desperate prostitution that are akin to rape: Sethe's exchange of sex for the engraving on her baby's tombstone (4–5, 134) and the Saturday girls' work at the slaughterhouse (203).

These incidents of rape frame Seine's explanation for killing her baby daughter. Sethe tries to tell the furious Beloved that death actually protected the baby from the deep despair that killed Baby Suggs, from "what Ella knew, what

Stamp saw and what made Paul D tremble" (251): horrific experiences and memories of rape. Whites do "not just work, kill, or maim you, but dirty you," Sethe tells Beloved, "Dirty you so bad you [can't] like yourself anymore." Sethe passionately insists that she protected her beloved daughter and also herself from "undreamable dreams" in which "a gang of whites invaded her daughter's private parts, soiled her daughter's thighs and threw her daughter out of the wagon" (251). For Sethe, being brutally overworked, maimed, or killed is subordinate to the overarching horror of being raped and "dirtied" by whites; even dying at the hands of one's mother is subordinate to rape.

Notes

I thank Trudier Harris for commenting on several drafts of this essay and for the inspired suggestion that I consider Beloved as a succubus and rapist figure. I also thank Andrew Cousins, Jodi Cressman, John Jones, Catherine Nickerson, Julie Abraham, and Angelika Bammer. Above all. I am grateful to Nicole Cooley for offering insight and support at every stage of the writing.

1. Criticism on the novel has focused largely on Beloved's relation to memory and history. See esp. Smith, Mobley.

2. While some critics have compared Beloved to a succubus or vampire in passing, Trudier Harris alone focuses on Beloved as a demonic figure who feeds on Paul D and Sethe. According to Harris, Beloved enacts vengeance against those who would thwart her desire for her mother: against Sethe herself and against Paul D, who tries to exorcize the house. Harris depicts a contest between Paul D's masculine power and Beloved's feminine otherness, which is represented by her insatiable desire. In fact, Harris argues that Sethe is masculine insofar as motherhood is a "symbol of authority almost masculine in its absoluteness." Thus Beloved's life-threatening feeding aims to usurp Sethe's and Paul D's masculine sense of entitlement to "power over life and death" (158). Although Harris does not treat Beloved's attacks as enactments of sexual violence, she suggested that I do so.

3. One type included in sixteenth- and seventeenth-century Christian classifications of demons is the "night terror, female demons that attack sleeping men, children and women in child-bed to suck them of their vitality and blood" (Guiley 92). The vampire and the old hag are forms of the night terror.

4. In *American Folklore*, Richard M. Dorson writes that "the shape shifting witches who straddle their victims in bed are English not African creations" (185). Newbell Niles Puckett records the belief in these figures in a 1926 collection, *Folk Beliefs of the Southern Negro*. Regardless of their origins, the figures appear in African American literature, notably in Charles Chesnutt's *The Conjure Woman* (1899): "en dey say she went out ridin' de niggers at night, fer she wuz a witch 'sides bein' a cun-juh 'oman" (15).

5. In *Unclaimed Experience: Trauma, Narrative, and History*, Cathy Caruth defines trauma as an "overwhelming experience of sudden catastrophic events in which the response to the event occurs in the often delayed, uncontrollable repetitive appearance of hallucinations and other intrusive phenomena" (11). This repetition is a response to the sudden and "unassimilated nature" of the event. In nightmares the trauma experience is made available to the consciousness that could not initially "know" it (4).

NANCY JESSER ON VIOLENCE, HOME, AND COMMUNITY

The terms *home* and *community* are frequently uttered with reverence by feminists, non-feminists, and anti-feminists alike. These terms and the spaces they conjure up are invoked as the cure to no end of social ills, from stress and malaise to crack addiction and corporate downsizing. Calls for the return to home and to community are both nostalgic and utopian. In "Coming Home," Carol Pearson discusses a feminist utopian narrative through which, " ... upon discovering a sexually egalitarian society, the narrators have a sense of coming home to a nurturing, liberating environment" (63). Other feminist theorists of utopia, such as Lucy Sargisson, worry that such blueprints represent an "inappropriate closure" to feminist utopian imaginings. Because domestic spaces have worked out for many women as places to be domesticated and/or to be a domestic, it is not surprising that most have mixed feelings about a structure that contains the often unfulfilled dream of possession and the lived experience of servitude. *Beloved*, a novel published during the domestic retrenchments and anti-feminist "backlash" of the 1980s, shows both the dystopian and utopian properties of the space named "home" and the people named "community." Morrison, through a complex interweaving of peopled spaces, shows how homes and communities serve as places to gather strength, formulate strategy, and rest, even as they are insufficient to the task of "solving" institutional and social ills.

In a process of personal and social transformation, *Beloved*'s spaces and times change through geographical and structural movement and through storytelling. Narrative processes are linked to spatial formations and communal configurations. Morrison's simultaneous working through of history and memory by describing bodies and social structures makes the novel useful not only for projects of remembrance and revision, but also for building new social configurations of family and kin. The role the ghost-daughter's body plays as a site for memory, desire, and history has been discussed in depth by many critics, but she/it is not the only embodied site in the novel at which memory and desire meet. The dwellings and places the characters move through and escape to become at times fixed containers of memory and desire, and at times spaces where boundaries between selves are softened, making possible the gatherings and joinings necessary for emancipatory struggles. When softer, they provide emotional and physical sustenance and can be built onto, accommodating gatherings.

Because the novel is a meditation on transformations of body and soul, it is necessary to mark the process of how spaces become hardened as well as how they may be softened again. Places in *Beloved* are made hard discursively and architecturally, marked off by the law, by walls, or by armed guards. They can also be open or be made open: fluid, dynamic, and partially or temporarily invisible to the law. What is important, however, is not recognizing or describing a space, or categorizing it, but charting the interactions between spaces and charting the processes of their hardening or softening.

The demands of self-protection and home make it impossible to rely entirely on "open" spaces, for they carry their own vulnerabilities. The rented house 124 Bluestone plays a crucial role in marking the possibilities and limits of transformations of spaces Morrison's characters inhabit. Possibilities, and the shutting down of possibilities, develop through interactions and processes. For example, the pre-apocalyptic 124 Bluestone (before Sethe takes the handsaw to her children) is a softened space in which the African-American community of Cincinnati meets and exchanges information and food. The post-apocalyptic 124 (after "the Misery") has become hardened, albeit ironically more "alive" in its resentment of intrusion and change. Through Denver's going out into the community and the exchange of food, she and the home become open to change and community intervention. The story contained in *Beloved* unfolds this process of memorialization and change, a process too complex to be easily diagramed or mapped. The story itself, as complex and unavoidable as weather, embodies a system and process by which houses, which are born out of violence and (repeated) trauma, which preserve memory and history, can be transformed into homes where violence need not be the only source of connection. Against and alongside the relations annealed by violence and domination, new affinities emerge, held together through exchanged material and spiritual sustenance.

Furthermore, when the home or the community becomes so hardened that passing from one to the other is difficult, if not impossible, then these spaces lose some of their power as catalysts for larger social transformations. Because chattel slavery, colonization, and racism penetrated every moment in U.S. history, there is a sense in which all homes are haunted by violence and trauma. To paraphrase Baby Suggs, there isn't a home in the U.S. (and perhaps America proper) not haunted by a "Negro's grief." It is Morrison's insistence on this widespread haunting that makes *Beloved* a useful place to investigate the troubled history of domestic spaces. The home is a place where horror becomes embodied, and where sustaining human connections can be found. The very walls and doors of the house can stymie interventions by the community, or facilitate them. (...)

124 Bluestone

The house to which Sethe and her family escape is owned by white abolitionists and rented to Baby Suggs. Nevertheless, Baby Suggs and Sethe create in it a space the interior of which is designed to promote warmth and provide sustenance, both to the family and to the community. Momentarily, the house is successful in providing a protected space for the community to gather with the family. But when the yard is invaded by slavery's institutional forces, triggering Sethe's desperate actions, the house becomes both an unapproachable and inescapable space—hard. While the present of the novel is located in 124, the house is haunted by the specter of reliving the past. Incursions into the yard and house by the past, whether brought by Paul D or Schoolteacher, cause breakdowns. Some of these breakdowns result in a hardening of the line between the yard and the world, some in an increased permeability.

The house and its relation to the community change drastically from when Baby Suggs lives there alone until the time of Paul D's arrival. Located in disputed territory, 124 Bluestone is caught between the claims of past scripts and the imagined possibilities of a new story. The past lives in the house, haunts it, and shields itself from being unwritten, re-written, or forgotten. The relationship of the characters to the past is conflicted, because it is pleasurable to remember connections through reminiscences, such as the caresses of Beloved and the memories of Sweet Home that "rolled themselves out in shameless beauty" (6). These memories, however, do not account for the pain that emanates from the house's being a site for the contested past, and a site wholly absorbed by the past—suspended, caught up in a protracted and "perfunctory battle" (4) with a ghost that saps all the energy of the living. Sethe's resistance to reliving the past has cast her into a kind of limbo, with no judgment and no forgiveness. In this way, *Beloved* is about joining together the stories of the past, making it impossible for them to be relived, and writing a new story into being.

124 Bluestone is both a good place to escape to and a "way station" on that journey (163). For Baby Suggs and Sethe it is the better place at the end of the journey, bought by Halle's labor, and perhaps life, and by Sethe's suffering. The cost of such a journey is dear, because the institution of slavery makes it so, and it is the ex-slaves who must pay. Garner's payment of Baby Suggs's settlement fee is added on to the debt that Halle must pay. Nevertheless, Baby Suggs acknowledges the value of the place where she is. Knowing that value, she turns the house into a beacon calling for and helping with the freeing of other black people:

124 had been a cheerful, buzzing house where Baby Suggs, holy, loved, cautioned, fed, chastised, soothed. Where not one but two pots simmered on the stove; where the lamp burned all night long. Strangers rested there while children tried on their shoes. Messages were left there, for whoever needed them was sure to stop in one day soon. (86)

124 is the nerve center and the heart of the black community. To insure that it will be the kind of space that will be open, Baby Suggs changes the structure of the white-owned house by making the kitchen indoors "like a cabin." Baby Suggs, who draws the community together with her preaching in the Clearing, maintains her doctrine of openness, grace, and love for every black woman, man, and child.

But her efforts to bring home her "scattered" family fail; slavery's systematic erasure of identity is too thorough for her to combat alone. So Baby Suggs opens her house and her heart to the whole community. The people take advantage of this, but her efforts are stymied by the invasion of this space by white people trying to return Sethe and her babies to the unbearable past. Her efforts are also stymied by the house's relation to the community; despite Baby Suggs's efforts to transform it into a cabin, it remains a "house with two floors and a well" (137). Her very generosity makes them furious. The blessings and Baby Suggs's sharing of these blessings set her apart even as they brought the community together in her yard, or at the Clearing. Baby Suggs works limitations—she "didn't approve of extra. 'Everything depends on knowing how much,' she said, and 'Good is knowing when to stop'" (86). Like the Hi Man she enacts this wisdom to the benefit of the community. And she is uneasy with the spontaneous celebration that erupts at Sethe's arrival.

At the party, the pies made by Baby Suggs are added to by the donations of the community, until there is too much food eaten and enjoyed. The four pies with which the feast begins are made from Stamp Paid's gift of blackberries, but they soon become eight. This generation of food, brought by the whole community and eaten to excess by the whole community, suddenly becomes a source of violent reaction, forcing a breakdown in solidarity. The community, though itself the source of the food, shapes it into a story about rivaling divine miracles and prideful generosity:

> Loaves and fishes were His powers—they did not belong to an ex-slave who had probably never carried one hundred pounds to the scale, or picked okra with a baby on her back. Who had never been lashed by a ten-year-old whiteboy as God knows they had. Who had not even escaped slavery—had in fact, been bought out of it by a doting son and *driven* to the Ohio river in a wagon—free papers folded between her breasts (driven by the very man who had been her master, who also paid her resettlement fee—name of Garner), and rented a house with two floors *and* a well from the Bodwins.... It made them furious. They swallowed baking soda, the morning after, to calm the stomach violence caused by the bounty, the reckless generosity on display at 124. Whispered to each other in the yards about fat rats, doom and uncalled-for pride. (137)

Suddenly, the very openness and generosity, which demanded a structural change in the white-owned two-story house, become the source of Baby Suggs's isolation from the community. The "talking low" which had occurred within 124 is transformed into whispered resentments:

> Too much, they thought. Where does she get it all, Baby Suggs, holy? Why is she and hers always the center of things? How come she always knows exactly what to do and when? Giving advice, passing messages, healing the sick, hiding fugitives, loving, cooking, cooking, loving, preaching, singing, dancing and loving everybody like it was her job and hers alone. (137)

Of course, the simple answer to the question "Where does she get it all?" is from the community. It is their own generosity that has provided the excess of food. But they see Baby Suggs as a locus of blessings, of realized dreams—getting her family out, getting out herself. Even though she turns her blessings into gifts for the community and provides a space for the necessary work of getting others out, the fact of these blessings creates a separation between her and the community. Though she tries to rebuild the house she has received to be a cabin, it stubbornly remains a two-story house—and hers alone. From this separation, violence is enabled.

For twenty-eight days Sethe experiences this paradise, this utopia, this house fully alive with no need to "take the ugly out." She has friends over; she is bathed and tended for the injuries she has sustained on her journey; she can love her children properly; and she can converse as part of a larger black community about matters of national as well as personal importance—such as the Fugitive Slave Act. The moment of destruction for the utopia happens with the confluence of two events: One is an invasion from the outside, and one a disruption of the community fabric. That 124 is set apart from the community because of its blessings and "reckless" generosity makes it more vulnerable. The invasion of 124 by the white people of Sweet Home, who are trying to re-cast Sethe and her children into their role as slaves, results in a paroxysm of violence.

When the four horsemen approach Sethe's house, the usual system of warning has broken down, after and through the party to celebrate Sethe's arrival and the survival of Denver. Stamp Paid later interprets this double lapse:

> He was going to tell him [Paul D] that, because he thought it was important: why he and Baby Suggs both missed it. And about the party too, because that explained why nobody ran on ahead; why nobody sent a fleet-footed son to cut 'cross a field soon as they saw the four horses in town hitched for watering while the riders asked questions. Not Ella, not John, not anybody ran down or to Bluestone Road, to say some new whitefolks with the Look just rode in. The righteous Look every Negro learned to recognize along with his ma'am's tit. Like a flag hoisted, this righteousness telegraphed and announced the faggot, the whip, the fist, the lie, long before it went public. Nobody warned them, and he'd always believed it wasn't the exhaustion from a long day's gorging that dulled them, but some other thing—like, well, like meanness—that let them stand aside, or not pay attention, or tell themselves somebody else was probably bearing the news already to the house on Bluestone Road where a pretty woman had been living for almost a month. Young and deft with four children one of which she delivered herself the day before she got there and who now had the full benefit of Baby Suggs' bounty and her big old heart. Maybe they just wanted to know if Baby really was special, blessed in some way they were not. (157)

Prophecy and the reading of the signs have failed in this instance. Stamp Paid and Baby Suggs are looking in the wrong direction, not attending to the signs. However, the more severe breakdown is the lack of solidarity—something born out of jealousy of others' blessings, and by naming those blessings and that generosity "pride." So the blessed can be excluded from the community of the less blessed, not yet blessed, or never to be blessed. Perhaps it is damaging to emancipatory movements that individuals' successes in escaping or avoiding harm isolate them, putting some into a safer space. This place enables a new exclusionary boundary to be erected. If someone moves into that new territory, then the community has two choices. Either make the boundaries flexible enough—cut off the chain that has bound them together, and allow the connection to exist on a metaphoric level—or re-assert the group identity based on being the unblessed, the oppressed, cutting the blessed individual out of the loop.

Ironically, being outside the community leaves Sethe and her family open to assault by the enforcers of the system of oppression that created the situation of being unblessed for the entire community. This leaves Sethe at once part of the community—because she has now been robbed of her blessing—but also outside of it, doubly unblessed. She is ostracized because of the actions she takes in the face of the assault that was in some part enabled by the community's failure to include her. The correct reading of the signs and a response to the threat from white people must be above the notions of desert or the system of signals will fail, endangering the blessings achieved by the concerted efforts of that same community. The community must work toward emancipation and toward the maintenance of emancipation, taking into account different attainments of grace—not risking those blessings attained to ensure an equality of oppression, an equality of suffering, and an equal portion of pain.

124 is transformed from the vibrant, "buzzing" nexus of the community to a house isolated from the outside and constricted from the inside. Once caught in the flux of life, the midst of journeys, communications, and sharing, 124 is hurled out of time to become a fixed, timeless world trapped on the border of death. The house is filled to such an extent with the spiteful ghost that "there was no room for any other thing or body" (39). The openness, the lack of constrictions and restrictions that made 124 the way station and message center, is reversed by the apocalyptic moment. The achievement of this apocalypse is a world out of time, fixed and fixing for all its inhabitants. When Sethe attempts to kill her children rather then see them brought back into slavery, Morrison clearly

points to Revelations—four horseman come riding down the road and enter the yard (148). The day of reckoning comes in the form of a tremendous violence, the flowing of blood, and a disruption of the maternal relationship that suggests the upheavals of judgment Day. The unleashing of Sethe's wrath is like that of the God of righteousness. She has been betrayed not only by the evil of white people and the world they rule, but also by the pride of her own people, who turn their backs and worship false idols.

After Sethe's actions, she enters a living death, signified by her blood-coated dress, which stiffens "like rigor mortis" (153). She awaits a resurrection, tries to propel her family to the other side, but the apocalypse fails to secure this paradise. The world has become a bad, unnatural place. Horrible upheavals of the natural occur, and Sethe sets out to destroy history as white people have written it. Her chosen people—her "'best things'" (272)—will not be required to live out the history assigned to them. The claims of the past must be shattered. Sethe tries to "out hurt the hurter" (234), to disrupt the narrative by employing the outrageous: love in the form of a handsaw. "She just flew. Collected every bit of life she had made, all the parts of her that were precious and fine and beautiful, and carried, pushed, dragged them through the veil, out, away, over there where no one could hurt them. Over there. Outside this place, where they would be safe" (163).

Again, Sethe has rewritten her destiny, escaped the role assigned to her and her children, but at what cost? Sethe's choice has propelled them out of history into a "timeless present." But she must ask the question, "'How bad is the scar?'" She says that it was not for her to know what could be worse, only to escape from what was known as worse. In her recollection of the events to Paul D, after he proclaims her act of mistaken identity, of not knowing "where the world stopped and she began," Sethe counters, "'They ain't at Sweet Home. Schoolteacher ain't got em....'" Paul D again counters, "'Maybe there's worse,'" to which Sethe replies, "'It ain't my job to know what's worse. It's my job to know what is and to keep them away from what I know is terrible'" (165).

And it is terrible. Her daughter is dead, her sons run away, and Denver is trapped in a kind of other world with Sethe. But Baby Suggs "could not approve or condemn Sethe's 'rough choice'" (180). The choices of all the mothers have been rough. And the boundaries of property and the possibilities of "imagined grace" in which she had faith are violated and repudiated in one moment: "The heart that pumped out love, the mouth that spoke the Word, didn't count. They came into her yard anyway" (180). Baby Suggs's new and last prophetic message to give to the world—now shrunk to Sethe and Denver—is "that there was no bad luck in the world but whitepeople. 'They don't know when to stop'" (104). The lesson that they could "come into the yard" at will is a devastating one for Baby Suggs, since she had restructured the space rented to her and transformed the Clearing into a place where grace could be imagined. As long as white people set the limits, African American attempts to transform their houses, their communities, and their minds into safe, open spaces remain subject to a re-assertion of the narrative of slavery.

The world is so imbued and shot through with white power that color remains the only harmless thing. Paul D calls Sethe on the danger of internalizing the definer's definitions: "'You got two feet, Sethe, not four'" (165). She may be enacting the role described by Schoolteacher and written down by him with the ink of her own making. The jungle created by white people, the evil created by slavery invades even the most carefully attended barriers. The "fence with a gate that somebody was always latching and unlatching in the time when 124 was busy as a way station" is "pulled down" by white boys who "yanked up the posts and smashed the gate leaving 124 desolate and exposed at the very hour when everybody stopped dropping by." Once exposed and isolated from the community, the house that was once the lamp on the hill has become "a breastplate of darkness" (163). The safety secured for its inhabitants has cost not only lives, but the future as well.

When Paul D arrives he brings both the Sweet Home past and the future with him. As he enters the possessed house, passing through its bloody veil of light, he disrupts its timelessness and isolation. His coming disrupts the physical spaces of the house. He "broke up the place, making room, shifting it [the ghost], moving it over to someplace else, then standing in the place that he had made" (39). Like Baby Suggs, he tries to adjust the house physically to account for problems that are spiritual and political. He shifts the ghost from occupying the house to occupying a body. Like Baby Suggs's structural changes, Paul D's cannot remedy the facts of the case—whether it is the size of the house, who owns it, or the fact that it is the site of a bloody incident. Before Paul D exorcises the spirit, Denver tries to tell him that the possession is not the source of their isolation—a comfortable fiction Sethe supports. She cries, "'It's not the house. It's us. And it's you'" (14). The displacement provides a temporary respite from the possession. The very same day that Paul D takes Sethe and Denver to the Carnival for a first venture off the property and first social event since the Misery, the ghost takes on its body—the mysterious Beloved.[8] The haunt becomes flesh, and Paul D has no power to displace her. Rather, it is she who "moves" him gradually out of 124, securing her space, taking over the present and shutting out the future.

The past which Paul D brings to 124 demands a new, painful writing of the past. Yet this threading together of stories allows for the fabric of their two lives to be joined into a potentially sheltering cloth in which the past is reworked into the present and into the future. But as is true of all the blessings in this novel that seek to displace the haunting pains of one past, a new kind of haunting emerges. Blessings cannot supplant or displace the terrible; it abides. Paul D "beat the spirit away the very day he entered her house and no sign of it since. A blessing, but in its place he brought another kind of haunting" (96). The story she made up about Halle and Sweet Home was integrated into her present. With Paul D's additions to the story, the past itself is changed. She now finds the memory of Halle's face smeared with butter and clabber. His being broken by the sight of his wife assaulted by teenage boys becomes part of her story. Sethe and Paul D cannot secure the future for each other because neither has yet integrated their whole pasts into their presents. They have not reckoned with the dead or their own deadness. Paul D's is locked in a tobacco box in his chest, and Sethe's demands attention like a spoilt or needy child.

Beloved's takeover of 124 secures its total isolation. As soon as Sethe understands who Beloved is, Beloved's claim on her and hers is total. Sethe no longer goes to work; she attends to Beloved's wishes. Denver—who once stood between her Sweet Home past and her 124 past—tries to make claims on both Beloved as a sister and Sethe as a mother, but she is gradually shut out of the relationship. But first there is a fusion of all three (a moment so pleasurable that the most basic connections to life, like eating, are set aside). In an attempt to take the "ugly" out of the past and to redeem her handsaw love, Sethe expends everything she has to surround Beloved with sweetness and finery. The three ice skate, drink cocoa, dress up in bright colors and ribbons. As though directly contrary to Baby Suggs's dictum, they do everything to excess. Yet the excess proffered Beloved leads to privation for Sethe and Denver. Beloved swallows everything, absorbing them into her ever larger body.

Two possibilities for these pasts are Beloved's two dreams of "exploding, and being swallowed" (133). The past either erupts into the present and threatens to re-write itself—as in the coming of Schoolteacher to 124. Or it is swallowed and made part of the living in a sacramental way. To combat her fate, Beloved possesses Sethe and Denver; their identities become increasingly dispersed only to coalesce around Beloved and her whims. In the four chapters that form the lyric heart of the book, Sethe and Denver lay claim to Beloved; Beloved lays claim to Sethe; and finally (in the fourth chapter) the pronouns slip from person to person until the boundaries are effaced. The *Is* and *yous* and the subjects of the sentences are barely distinguishable, no longer separated grammatically or typographically. These lyric-voice chapters conclude with a joining—"You are mine, you are mine, you are mine" (217)— and the possession is complete. The haunt has achieved its purpose of crowding out all other possible imaginings. Sethe's, Beloved's, and Denver's relative positions in time are lost; their separate histories, their private thoughts, their terrible stories, and their bodies are fused, leaving Denver and Sethe possessed by all the dead and lost, all the Beloveds. And when Beloved possesses all she knows to want, she "invented desire" (240).

While 124 "exhausts" itself in total isolation, Paul D sorts through the fragments of Sethe's story, the newspaper article, Stamp Paid's view, and his own knowledge of Sethe. It is through him and through Stamp Paid's aborted visit that the black community first hears about Beloved's arrival. 124 and the community are still estranged, but the goings-on are acknowledged. It is for Denver to break up the estrangement. For her 124 was the whole known world. It is also her own worse place. Until she can imagine that the future could hold no worse for her, she cannot form her plan to leave the yard. Denver's fear, which is the fear she learned from her mother, is that the past will write itself into her future. And yet not to risk her own apocalyptic moment of resistance to a repeating past is to risk losing her mother and eventually herself. Sethe and Denver exist within an entropic system headed toward collapse: The past is obliterated and the present is starved; Beloved's strength is growing, and Sethe's and ultimately Denver's size is diminished. Only in this situation will Denver risk going "out there where there were places in which things so bad had happened that when you went near them it would happen again. Like Sweet Home where time didn't pass and where, like her mother said, the bad was waiting for her as well" (243–44). The vortex that Denver fears is precisely the vortex that Sethe approached and denied, hurling her instead into an inescapable relationship with her own past. The rough choice that Denver must make is between risking entrapment in a narrative written by the white power structure, a fate ready and waiting for her, and being swallowed up into a closed and exhausting relationship with that past that has marked and nourished her—as she drank her own sister's blood.

The other abiding spirit, that of Baby Suggs, reaches Denver with her final prophecy. The solution to the dilemma is no solution at all. It is to "know"[9] that there is no absolute "defense" against the claims of a competing and brutal narrative that may cast you in the role of victim. Armed only with this knowledge, Denver must "go on out of the yard" (244). Baby Suggs had learned that the yard, while it seems protected and protective, is itself no defense. For Baby Suggs, hell isn't others; others are the only defense. When Denver leaves the yard and approaches Lady Jones, the teacher of the "unpicked" (247), she sets into motion a process that brings sustenance to 124, and begins to re-integrate Denver into the larger community through a network of generosity.

Denver's ventures out of the yard re-link 124 to the black community. She is "strengthened by the gifts of food" and now has two "lives," her "outside life" and her "home life" (250). The story cannot end until these two lives are re-integrated. This re-integration happens through a confluence of events— Denver's commitment to working for the Bodwins outside 124 and outside the black community, far into the "whitepeople" world, and the convergence of black women to exorcize the ghost. Once the house and its inhabitants are brought back into the compass of the community by Denver's escape, the boundary established on the day Sethe hurled the world out can be re-negotiated. The reclamation of 124, like the escape from Alfred, comes through a concerted effort.

Ella, the practical woman, leads a group prayer at the edge of the property. Participants "bring what they could and what they believed would work" (257). Denver waits to go out into a risky world, one in which the "bad places" wait to re-write you into their story. A white man is again coming into the yard, and surrounded by an army of women, he enters it. Sethe sees the past reaching out to pull her back in. This time, however, she doesn't disrupt the narrative by hurting her own—what was made vulnerable and hurtable by the enemy—instead she strikes out at Mr. Bodwin, the unwitting abolitionist, who understands how he is seen by whites as a "bleached nigger," but is unaware of how he is a "man without skin" to the ex-slave, Sethe. She repeats the apocalyptic moment, but here reverses the role of destroyer/unproducer and creator/producer, putting Bodwin in the role of victim. Denver steps in to disrupt the whole unfolding narrative—which threatens to cut the filaments that she has woven between herself and the world outside. The world to which she has chosen to be connected is clearly not without risk, or without "tests and trials." Denver has taken over the writing of her future and crossed out of a yard that hemmed her in, creating space in which to make connections.

Sethe is still tied to her ghost and to her method of changing the narrative, using a violence we, like Baby Suggs, can neither condemn nor approve. In the first coming of white people into her yard, she turns the violence against herself and her own, but she does not strike out at Schoolteacher. The constraints laid on her are his guns, and the weight of the law. In the second coming, she seeks to re-write her role as object of violence onto the agent, Mr. Bodwin. But part of the problem with this way of getting out of the oppressed position is that the person turned victim may not be the source of oppressive power. Sethe assigns to Mr. Bodwin a role based on the qualities of his skin, disrupting neither the racist modes of thinking nor the white supremacist structures of the larger society.

It is important here to recall that Sethe's killing of the "crawling already? baby" is not the only infanticide in the novel, nor is it the only instance of a "rough choice." The woman who cares for Sethe when she is a child tells her that her mother killed all the babies conceived on the slave ship, as well as those of white men, and that Sethe was not killed because she was a child of love. This is not to say that Morrison is suggesting that the way to escape oppressive structures is this kind of self-destructive behavior. Rather we are bound, to some degree, to act and make rough choices within the narratives that we live. The specificity of historical moments allows for and demands certain and, at times, mixed-up choices. None are choices for all time, and none are apocalyptic enough to end the history in which we find ourselves. But, Morrison suggests, we bear a kind of haunting from these choices that in turn haunts the future. Sethe's mother's choices and her own choices haunt Denver, and Denver must live with the consequences of her mother's choice, but not be absorbed by this past. Her future is another rough choice to get to a "better life" that is not her "other one," the one paralyzed and bound by her mother's choice. When Denver takes control of the unfolding scene by wrestling the weapon from her mother's hand, she makes it possible for the past narrative to explode, releasing Sethe into a rest, and a small clearing of space in which to live out the rest of her life. Her connections to the present and to the future are tenuous and airy. The possibilities for Beloved's fate were being "exploded" or "swallowed." By this time, Sethe has swallowed many of the pieces of the past. Paul D has taken his memories and made them a part of his present. He and Sethe know each other and know each other's pasts. She can leave him his manhood, and he can leave her humanity. It is all exploded and swallowed. Paul D ends with an assertion about the "need" for a future, and to that end he is ready to join his story to hers. What each has suffered has to become joined with all the other narratives of suffering. How each has escaped has to become joined with all the other stories of escape. The description of the scars has to join with the descriptions of bathings and healings.

Notes

8. I concur with Osagie's reading of the "complementarity" of the differing readings of Beloved's "true" identity, either as Sethe's daughter's ghost or a "captive from Africa" (see House). For a discussion of the "ghost," see Horvitz and Rigney. Other critics relate the fleshly ghost to a West African figure, the *ogbanje*, a demon/child who seeks to be born again and again, and is therefore marked by the mother so that it will be recognized on its return.

9. Susan E. Babbitt's article provides an interesting reading of Drucilla Cornell and Morrison. She explores the relationship between questions of knowledge and questions of identity (and subjectivity). According to Babbitt, epistemological questions occur within conceptual frameworks, and transformations in understanding and knowledge cannot be "acquired any other way than by bringing about certain conditions or ways of being.... Individuals ... have to act and be in specific ways in order to proceed as human beings" (16–17).

J. Brooks Bouson on Sethe's "Best Thing"

As Morrison focuses on the physical oppression and also the shame-humiliation suffered by the slaves, she underscores the link between trauma and shame in *Beloved*, showing that, as trauma investigators have concluded, the deliberate and sadistic infliction of injury can induce unbearable and chronic feelings of shame. Judith Herman, for example, discusses how victims of repeated trauma, such as those held in captivity, may suffer from a "contaminated identity" and be preoccupied with "shame, self-loathing, and a sense of failure" (*Trauma* 94). Ronnie Janoff-Bulman similarly remarks that "human-induced victimizations are … characterized as humiliating," since the victims, who are "overpowered by another, a malevolent perpetrator," feel not only "helpless" but also "sullied and tarnished in the process" (80). The lethal impact of shame has also been commented on by Lawrence Langer in his studies of Holocaust victims. The fact that some survivors of the Holocaust have insisted that the humiliations they suffered in the concentration camps were "often worse than death" points to the toxicity of what Langer calls "humiliated memory," an "intense form of uncompensating recall" that reanimates the "governing impotence of the worst moments" of a debilitating past (77, 83–84).

Plagued by intrusive memories, trapped in a fragmented world of repetition, Morrison's ex-slave character, Sethe, is driven by the need to reveal and conceal as she struggles to both remember and not remember, to say and not say the painful secrets of her slavery past. While Sethe feels that she must keep the past "at bay" (42), she remains haunted by her traumatic and humiliated rememories. For "her brain was not interested in the future. Loaded with the past and hungry for more, it left her no room to imagine, let alone plan for, the next day" (70). Deliberately using a fragmented and repetitive narrative structure to convey the disrupted, obsessive world of the trauma victim, Morrison circles around and around the shameful secrets that haunt her character: Sethe's paralyzing and dirtying memories of the physical and psychic assaults on her humanity she suffered as a slave, memories that are too awful to speak of directly and can only be told incrementally, in bits and pieces. In *Beloved*, Morrison also dramatizes the inherent difficulty of the trauma testimony. As Cathy Caruth has remarked, the fact that "in trauma the greatest confrontation with reality may also occur as an absolute numbing to it" leads to the paradox of trauma: that its "overwhelming immediacy ... produces its belated uncertainty" ("Introduction" 5). Thus, there is a "crisis of truth" in the trauma testimony, for traumatized individuals carry "an impossible history within them, or they become themselves the symptom of a history that they cannot entirely possess" ("Introduction" 5, 4). (...)

That Sethe kills her infant daughter to prevent her from being defined as racially inferior and animalistic—and thus from being dirtied—underscores the historical shaming of African slave women that Morrison is intent on exposing in *Beloved*. Tracing the historical and cultural origins of the essentialist racist discourse that constructed the African woman as animallike, Patricia Collins notes how "[b]iological notions of race and gender prevalent in the early nineteenth century which fostered the animalistic icon of Black female sexuality were joined by the appearance of a racist biology incorporating the concept of degeneracy." There were also critical economic factors at work in treating blacks as animals, for animals could be "economically exploited, worked, sold, killed, and consumed," treatment that slave women became "susceptible to" (171). The "externally defined, controlling image of the breeder woman" created during slavery also served white economic interests. "By claiming that Black women were able to produce children as easily as animals, this objectification of Black women as the Other provided justification for interference in the reproductive rights of enslaved Africans. Slaveowners wanted enslaved Africans to 'breed' because every slave child born represented a valuable unit of property, another unit of labor, and, if female, the prospects for more slaves" (76).

While nineteenth-century Southern society exalted white motherhood, slave women, in the words of Angela Davis, were "not mothers at all." Because they were "classified as 'breeders' as opposed to 'mothers,' their infant children could be sold away from them like calves from cows" (7). The African slave woman, who was subjected to an "institutionalized pattern of rape" under the slavery system (Davis 23), also became associated with illicit sexuality, giving rise to the shaming stereotype of the black Jezebel. The "controlling image" of the Jezebel, explains Collins, "originated under slavery when Black women were portrayed as ... 'sexually aggressive wet nurses.'" By relegating black women to the sexually aggressive category, the Jezebel image provided "a powerful rationale for the widespread sexual assaults by white men typically reported by Black slave women." Moreover, "If Black slave women could be portrayed as having excessive sexual appetites, then increased fertility should be the expected outcome. By suppressing the nurturing that African-American women might give their own children which would strengthen Black family networks, and by forcing Black women to work in the field or 'wet nurse' white children, slaveowners effectively tied the controlling images of Jezebel and Mammy to the economic exploitation inherent in the institution of slavery" (77).

In examining in *Beloved* the economic and sexual exploitation of slave women and the shaming racist constructions of slave women as hyperembodied and hypersexualized, Morrison reflects the recent endeavors in the developing scholarly study of black women's history to challenge the "old image" of the slave woman as "collaborator with white oppression" and to show that the slave woman was "doubly oppressed in that both her productive and reproductive capacities were used and abused" (Morton 144). The female slave, as Barbara Omolade aptly puts it, was a "fragmented commodity," whose "back and muscle were pressed into field labor," whose "hands were demanded to nurse and nurture the white man and his family as domestic servant," whose "vagina, used for his sexual pleasure, was the gateway to the womb, which was his place of capital investment" (354). In *Beloved*, the doubly oppressed Baby

Suggs, whose years as a slave "busted her legs, back, head, eyes, hands, kidneys, womb and tongue," is forced to have eight children by six fathers (87). What Baby Suggs calls the "nastiness of life" is the shock she feels on discovering that "nobody stopped playing checkers just because the pieces included her children." Out of all her children, her son, Halle, is the one Baby is allowed to keep the longest—twenty years. Halle is given to Baby "to make up for *hearing* that her two girls, neither of whom had their adult teeth, were sold and gone and she had not been able to wave goodbye. To make up for coupling with a straw boss for four months in exchange for keeping her third child, a boy, with her—only to have him traded for lumber in the spring of the next year and to find herself pregnant by the man who promised not to and did. That child she could not love and the rest she would not" (23). In focusing on the doubly oppressed slave woman and slavery's disruption of the mother–child bond, *Beloved* also dramatizes that the slave woman's "resistance tactics" to "forced miscegenation" included infanticide, as recent historians have pointed out (Morton 144).[3] Ella, for example, who spends her puberty in a house where she is "shared" by a father and son, whom she calls "the lowest yet," delivers but refuses to nurse the "hairy white thing, fathered by 'the lowest yet,'" and thus the infant lives only five days (256, 258–59). Similarly, Sethe's mother—who is hanged when Sethe is a child—is raped many times by members of the white crew on the slave ship that brings her to America. Resisting her sexual exploitation, she throws away the child from the crew and also the other children fathered by other whites, keeping only Sethe, who is fathered by the black man she willingly put her arms around.

Affectively and cognitively invested in ripping the veil historically drawn over proceedings too terrible to relate in *Beloved*, Morrison details the oppression of slave women as she tells the story of Sethe, who learns of the shaming power of the white definers: their power to define her as less than human. When the "iron-eyed" and proud Sethe first comes to Sweet Home as a thirteen-year-old, she is left alone by the men, allowed to "choose" one of them "in spite of the fact that each one would have beaten the others to mush to have her" (10). "Only my wool shawl kept me from looking like a haint peddling," Sethe remarks, describing the wedding dress she patches together from stolen fabric when she "marries" Halle, Baby Suggs's son. "I wasn't but fourteen years old, so I reckon that's why I was so proud of myself" (59). Yet even as *Beloved* describes Sethe's youthful pride, it also shows that she is implicitly shamed, objectified as the racial and sexual Other— as the animalistic breeder woman. "[M]inus women, fucking cows, dreaming of rape," the Sweet Home men wait for Sethe to select one of them (11). When Sethe and Halle have sex in the cornfield—Halle wanting "privacy" for Sethe but, instead, getting "public display"—the Sweet Home men, "erect as dogs," watch the corn stalks "dance at noon." To Paul D, the "jump ... from a calf to a girl wasn't all that mighty," nor was it the "leap Halle believed it would be" (26–27). Although Sethe has the "amazing luck of six whole years of marriage" to a man who fathers every one of her children, after the death of Garner and the arrival of schoolteacher, she learns of her value and function as a breeder slave woman, as "property that reproduced itself without cost" (23, 228).

"It was a book about us but we didn't know that right away," Sethe remarks as she recalls how schoolteacher asked the Sweet Home slaves questions and then wrote down what they said in his notebook with the ink Sethe mixed for him (37). Schoolteacher, despite his "pretty manners" and "soft" talking and apparent gentleness (36–37), is a cruel racist. A practitioner of the nineteenth-century pseudoscience of race, which included the systematic measurements of facial angles, head shapes, and brain sizes (see Stepan, "Race" 43, 45–47), schoolteacher is bent, as he makes his "scientific" inquiries, on documenting the racial inferiority of the Sweet Home slaves. At first Sethe is not concerned about schoolteacher's measuring string. "Schoolteacher'd wrap that string all over my head, 'cross my nose, around my behind. Number my teeth. I thought he was a fool," she recalls (191). Describing the biosocial investigation of racial difference in the nineteenth century, which was given "political urgency" by the abolitionist movement, Nancy Stepan notes how the "scientific" study of race served to "elevate hitherto unconsciously held analogies"—such as the long-standing comparison of blacks to apes—into "self-conscious theory" ("Race" 43, 42). A theory that codified the shaming of blacks and white contempt for the "lower" races, the study of racial differences functioned to give so-called scientific confirmation of the superiority (pride) of the higher and civilized white race and the inferiority (shame) of the lower and degenerate black race.[4]

Sethe, who initially thinks that schoolteacher is a fool, is humiliated on discovering the purpose of schoolteacher's measurements and observations when she overhears him instructing his pupils on how to scientifically describe her as a member of a lower race by listing her human traits on one side of the page and her animal traits on the other. In the essentialist racist discourse of schoolteacher, Sethe is constructed as animalistic: that is, as fundamentally and biologically different from white people. That the contempt of another has the power to degrade the individual's "value as a person" by equating the individual "with a debased, dirty thing—a derided and low animal"—and that the purpose of contempt is to instill in the individual a sense of "self-disgust and therefore shame at self-unworthiness" (Wurmser, *Mask* 81, Nathanson, *Shame and Pride* 129) is illustrated in this scene. The contemptuous racist discourse of schoolteacher engenders feelings of self-contempt in Sethe, who feels dirtied when she is suddenly exposed to the magnitude of schoolteacher's disgust for her race. The fact that this humiliating moment of exposure continues to haunt Sethe years later—that, indeed, she becomes caught up in a feeling trap of shame as she continues to replay this scene in her mind—reveals the depth of the shame she feels on learning of her designated role as the contemptible and debased racial inferior. Following her inscription into schoolteacher's shaming discourse on essential racial differences, Sethe feels blameworthy, believing that she has somehow collaborated with schoolteacher. "I made the ink.... He couldn't have done it if I hadn't made the ink," she later tells Paul D (271).

Despite her proud demeanor, the "quiet, queenly" (12) Sethe is a woman tormented by humiliated memories not only of how schoolteacher defined her as animallike but also of how his nephews treated her like an animal. Before Sethe, who is pregnant with Denver, is able to escape from Sweet Home, she has her milk stolen by schoolteacher's nephews. When Sethe learns from Paul D that her husband, Halle, watched this degrading spectacle and was consequently driven mad by what he had witnessed, her "rebellious" and "greedy" brain takes in this "hateful picture," adding it to her painful memory of this central shame event. "I am full God damn it of two boys with mossy teeth, one sucking on my breast the other holding me down, their book-reading teacher watching and writing it up.... Add my husband to it, watching, above me in the loft ... looking down on what I couldn't look at all.... There is also my husband squatting by the churn smearing the butter as well as its clabber all over his face because the milk they took is on his mind" (70). Objectified as the racial and sexual Other, Sethe is treated like a sexually aggressive wet nurse and mammy when schoolteacher's nephews sexually assault her in the barn, nursing from her breasts and stealing her milk. She also is treated like an animal, milked as if she were "the cow, no, the goat, back behind the stable because it was too nasty to stay in with the horses" (200). Afterward, she is beaten like an animal by schoolteacher's nephews for telling Mrs. Garner what has happened to her. Following schoolteacher's orders, the two boys dig a hole in the ground to protect the developing foetus—which is considered to be the property of the white slave owner—and then they brutally beat Sethe on her back with cowhide.[5] "Felt like I was split in two ... . Bit a piece of my tongue off when they opened my back. It was hanging by a shred. I didn't mean to. Clamped down on it, it come right off. I thought, Good God, I'm going to eat myself up" (202).

Escaping Sweet Home alone, the pregnant and traumatized Sethe gives birth to Denver on the "bloody side of the Ohio River" with the help of Amy Denver, a shamed white girl, the "raggediest-looking trash you ever saw" (31, 31–32). When Amy, who claims she is "good at sick things" (82), treats Sethe's injured back, she describes the pattern made by the seeping and pus-filled wounds as a chokecherry tree—a description that serves to aestheticize the shame and trauma of Sethe's situation. "It's a tree," Amy tells Sethe. "See, here's the trunk—it's red and split wide open, full of sap, and this here's the parting for the branches. You got a mighty lot of branches. Leaves, too, look like, and dern if these ain't blossoms. Tiny little cherry blossoms, just as white. Your back got a whole tree on it. In bloom" (79). Years later, when Paul D and Sethe are reunited at Sethe's haunted house, Paul D lovingly touches the "sculpture" of Sethe's scarred back, which is "like the decorative work of an ironsmith too passionate for display" (17). And yet after Paul D and Sethe make love, he thinks of "the wrought-iron maze he had explored" as a "revolting clump of scars" (21)—this change in Paul D's perception exemplary of the way the narrative alternates between providing an explicit and revolting depiction of slavery's atrocities and aestheticizing what it describes. Sethe's scarred back is a visible reminder of her traumatic abuse, both her physical violation and her psychic wounds, and it also concretizes her marked identity as the racially and stigmatized Other. The fact that even Paul D comes to react with revulsion to Sethe's scarred back points to the way that victims of extreme trauma and humiliation may be viewed by others as tainted and damaged. Thus, Paul D, even though he identifies with and honors Sethe's suffering, also perceives her, on some level, as an object of shame and disgust.

Despite the fact that Sethe is shamed when she is objectified as the sexualized breeder woman and the Jezebel-Mammy, that is, as the sexually aggressive wet nurse, she continues to identify herself primarily as a mother, taking deep pride in her fiercely protective mother love. Indeed, Sethe registers her resistance to the white slaveowner culture through her mothering and her desire to nurse her own children. "I had milk," Sethe recalls. "I was pregnant with Denver but I had milk for my baby girl. I hadn't stopped nursing her when I sent her on ahead.... Anybody could smell me long before he saw me. And when he saw me he'd see the drops of it on the front of my dress.... All I knew was I had to get my milk to my baby girl. Nobody was going to nurse her like me" (16). Also proud of her escape from Sweet Home, Sethe tells Paul D, "I did it. I got us all out. Without Halle too. Up till then it was the only thing I ever did on my own. Decided. And it came off right, like it was supposed to." Recalling her expansive feeling of pride, she remarks, "I was big, Paul D, and deep and wide and when I stretched out my arms all my children could get in between. I was *that* wide" (162). Commenting on how individuals evaluate their actions against the "yardstick" of the shame–pride axis, Donald Nathanson explains that while shame is associated with "incompetence, failure, or inadequacy," pride stems from the pleasure felt "in a moment of competence." The individual's "precarious sense of self" is balanced between shame and pride, between the "hoped-for *personal best*" and the "terribly feared *personal worst* that ... will trigger an avalanche of deadly shame" (*Shame and Pride* 20). Whereas there is a "wish to conceal" shame, there is a "tendency to broadcast" pride. But it is also the case that "in adult life pride is viewed with suspicion." Because it is associated with "vanity, foolishness, weakness, indeed becoming almost a synonym for narcissism, adult pride is dangerously close to the very shame that is supposed to be its opposite" ("Shame/Pride Axis" 184, 188). Just how dangerously close pride is to shame is revealed in the shame–pride drama that unfolds after Sethe's successful escape from Sweet Home and her arrival at Baby Suggs's home on the outskirts of Cincinnati.

Notes

3. Darlene Hine discusses three methods used by female slaves to resist their economic and sexual oppression: sexual abstinence, abortion, and infanticide. While there are only a "small number of documented cases" of infanticide, the fact that it happened at all is "significant" in Hine's view. Responding to Eugene Genovese's remark that "for the most part ... the slaves recognized infanticide as murder" and thus "courageously" attempted to raise their children "as best they could," Hine faults Genovese for not "acknowledging the motivations for infanticide offered repeatedly by the slave parents themselves. Far from viewing such actions as murder, and therefore indicating these as lack of love, slave parents who took their children's lives may have done so out of a higher form of love and a clearer

understanding of the living death that awaited their children under slavery" (125). Infanticide may also have resulted as a response to rape or forced pregnancy and sometimes slave children were used "as pawns in a power struggle between plantation owners and their slaves" (126). Steven Weisenburger comments that "when the infanticidal mother acts out the system's violent logic in the master's face, thus displaying anger and revenge against his class, she mirrors his violent politics in profoundly disruptive ways.... In such moments the dispossessed mother represents unutterable contradictions that the dominant culture must repress or mask" (263).

4. In *Degeneration, Culture, and the Novel*, William Greenslade remarks, "By the mid-nineteenth century racial biology had mapped out a 'science of boundaries between groups and the degenerations that threatened them when those boundaries were transgressed.' ... In contrast to industrious 'historic races' of northern Europe, certain races were cast as degenerate types. The biologist Cuvier identified the negro race as 'the most degraded human race whose form approaches that of the beast.' ... For the major race theorist of the nineteenth century, Comte de Gobineau (1816–1882), such was the necessity of keeping the races apart, that miscegenation and race-mingling would inevitably lead to degeneration and the extinction of civilization. For many race theorists, including Robert Knox and Charles Kingsley in Britain, the degenerate races were best off dead" (21-22).

Nancy Stepan, in "Biological Degeneration: Races and Proper Places," discusses the interest of racial biologists in the idea of racial types and their "proper places." "On the basis of analogies between human races and animal species, it was argued that races, like animal types, tended to be confined to definite localities of the earth." Not only did races have ties to particular geographical places, but movement out of their designated places "caused a 'degeneration.'" A common theme "sounded in the typological theory of racial degeneration" was "the degenerations caused by the movement of freed blacks into the geographical and social spaces occupied by whites and into the political condition of freedom" (99).

A "major concern" of American racial biologists was the "proper place" of blacks in the Americas, observes Stepan. "Most racial theorists in the United States shared, by the 1840s and 1850s, the typological orientation of the European scientists" (99–100). It was argued, for example, that "though Negroes fared well in the hotter, southern latitudes of the United States, north of forty degrees latitude they steadily deteriorated." After the Civil War and the freeing of the slaves, the "old belief that freed blacks were, of all blacks, the 'most corrupt, depraved, and abandoned element in the population,' was ... given a biological rationale" (101). "Freedom was an unnatural environment which removed constraints and plunged the Negro into 'natural' and innate excesses and indulgence of the racial appetites." Given freedom, blacks returned "to their primitive state of savagery and sexuality, revealing the ancient features of the race by a process of reversion" (102).

5. Angela Davis, in her discussion of the treatment of slave women as breeders and field workers, quotes from Moses Grandy's description of the floggings pregnant workers received for failing to complete the day's quota of work or for protesting their treatment:

> A woman who gives offense in the field, and is large in a family way, is compelled to lie down over a hole made to receive her corpulency, and is flogged with the whip or beat with a paddle, which has holes in it; at every stroke comes a blister. One of my sisters was so severely punished in this way, that labor was brought on, and the child was born in the field. This very overseer, Mr. Brooks, killed in this manner a girl named Mary. Her father and mother were in the field at that time. (Davis 9; quoted from the *Narrative of the Life of Moses Grandy. Late a Slave in the United States of America* [Boston: 1844].)

When pregnant women were treated with more leniency, writes Davis, "it was seldom on humanitarian grounds. It was simply that slaveholders appreciated the value of a slave child born alive in the same way that they appreciated the value of a newborn calf or colt" (9–10).

SUSAN BOWERS ON "REMEMORY"

Morrison shares with post-Holocaust Jewish artists the monumental difficulties attendant in depicting the victims of racial genocide. What Elie Wiesel has stated about the Holocaust applies to the slaughter of ten times as many Africans and African Americans as the six million Jews killed by Hitler (Morrison has said that 60 million is the smallest figure she had gotten from anyone for the number of slaves who died as a result of slavery [Angelo, 120]).

The Holocaust is not a subject like all the others. It imposes certain limits.... in order not to betray the dead and humiliate the living, this particular subject demands a special sensibility, a different approach, a rigor strengthened by respect and reverence and, above all, faithfulness to memory. (Wiesel, 38)

Betrayal would include sentimentalizing and thus trivializing the victims of slavery, rendering them merely pathetic and pitiable. Morrison does not do that. She dedicated *Beloved* to the "Sixty Million and More," and her novel conjures slaves back to life in many-dimensional characters with a full range of human emotions. They love and hate, sin and forgive, are heroic and mean, self-sacrificing and demanding. They endure incredible hardships to sustain relationships, but the inconceivable brutality and degradation which they experience fractures their communities and inflicts both physical and perhaps irreparable psychological damage on individuals.

One of the questions which *Beloved* asks is whether it is possible to transform unspeakably horrific experiences into knowledge. Is the magnitude of their horror too great to assimilate? Perhaps because the novel asks its readers, especially African Americans, to "dwell on the horror" which those rushing away from slavery could not, it addresses what happens when the magnitude of that horror is acknowledged, even suggesting how to survive the bringing into consciousness of what has lain hidden for so long. The struggle of *Beloved*'s characters to confront the effects of the brutality and to recover their human dignity, their selves "dirtied" by white oppression—to transform their experiences into knowledge—is presented in the form of a slave narrative that can be read as a model for contemporary readers attempting to engage these brutal realities. Slave narratives emphasize personal quest as a means of "wrest[ing] the black subject out of anonymity, inferiority and brutal disdain" (Willis, 213). *Beloved* combines the personal quest theme with the collective memory of racial brutality, for although apocalyptic literature features the destiny of the individual and personal salvation, its "overall perspective is still that of the community" (Russell, 27). (...)

"Rememorying" is what Morrison's characters call it, and it is the central activity in *Beloved*. Because of it the narrative moves constantly back and forth between past and present, mixing time inextricably, as memory escalates its battle against amnesia. The voice of the former slave "above all *remembering* his ordeal in bondage" can be "the single most impressive feature of a slave narrative" (Stepto, 1). The characters' rememorying in *Beloved* epitomizes the novel's purpose of conjuring up the spirits and experiences of the past and thus ultimately empowering both characters and readers. *Beloved* pairs the stories of a woman and a man, Sethe and Paul D. Sethe's name may be an allusion to Lethe, the spring of forgetfulness in Greek myth. The past that was too painful for either to remember alone can be recovered together: "Her story was bearable because it was his as well" (*Beloved*, 99). Their stories reveal that the worst brutality they have suffered "is less a single act than the systematic denial of the reality of black lives" (C. Davis, 323), the profound humiliation which both know can be worse than death:

> That anybody white could take your whole self for anything that came to mind. Not just work, kill, or maim you, but dirty you. (*Beloved*, 251)

Remembering is part of reversing the "dirtying" process that robbed slaves of self-esteem.

The concentration on the horrors of the past and present—the misuse of power, the cruelty and injustice—is characteristic of apocalyptic writing. However, the traditional apocalyptic anticipation of the messianic age—the time of freedom and redemption—is missing among these slaves and ex-slaves for whom hope has come to seem a cruel trick. The members of Paul D's chain gang try to destroy that part of themselves as they crush stone: "They killed the flirt whom folks called Life for leading them on" (*Beloved*, 109).

The typical format of the slave narrative is to trace the story of the individual's life in slavery, escape, and the journey to freedom (Willis, 220). What Morrison reveals is that the process must be repeated twice: first to leave physical enslavement by whites and the second time to escape the psychological trauma created by their brutality. The physical escapes of both Sethe and Paul D create the patterns for their psychological escapes: archetypal journeys of courage, descents into almost certain death, and rebirths into beauty and freedom. Sethe gives birth with the help of a young white girl when she reaches the Ohio River and thus freedom. Paul D is helped by Cherokees, who "describe the beginning of the world and its end and tell him to follow the tree flowers to the North and freedom" (112).

But the novel opens with characters still traumatized many years after their escapes from slavery. They are numb, almost incapable of emotion because they have suffered so deeply and seen such terror. Sethe and her daughter are literally haunted by the ghost of her murdered baby. Sethe is unable to feel; every morning she sees the dawn but never acknowledges its color. Paul D experiences his heart as a "tobacco tin lodged in his chest" (113), which holds the painful memories of his own past, the memories of one friend being burned to death, of others hanging from trees, his brothers being sold and taken away, of being tortured. "By the time he got to 124 nothing in this world could pry it open" (113). Paul D's arrival at 124, Sethe's home, 18 years after the two had last seen each other, begins their long and excruciating process of thawing frozen feeling.

Contemporary research on treatment for post-traumatic stress syndrome indicates that support and caring from others can help victims to heal, but that the most crucial part of healing is the unavoidable confrontation with the original trauma and feeling the pain again (Brown). *Beloved* enacts that theory. Sethe and Paul D are able to help each other to a point, but until they have intimate contact with the original pain and the feelings it created that had to be suppressed, they cannot be purged of its paralyzing effect.

What breaks open Paul D's tin heart and allows Sethe to see and love color again (color often appears in Morrison's fiction as a sign of the ability to feel) is Beloved's return from the dead, not as a ghost but a living being. She climbs fully dressed out of the water—perhaps representing the collective unconscious of African Americans—while, appropriately, Sethe, Paul D., and Sethe's daughter Denver are at a carnival (etymologically, "festival of flesh"). Beloved has "new skin, lineless and smooth" (*Beloved*, 50), no expression in her eyes, three thin scratches on her head where Sethe had held her head after severing her neck, and a small neck scar. Although Sethe does not consciously recognize her daughter for some time, her bladder fills the moment she sees her face and she voids "endless" water as if giving birth (*Beloved*, 51). For each of the three residents of 124—Sethe, Paul D and Denver—relating to Beloved addresses her or his most profound individual anguish, whatever lies at the core of each identity. For Sethe, it is mothering; for Paul D, his ability to feel, and for Denver, her loneliness. Their individual reactions to her reflect their respective voids and reveal their deepest selves. (...)

Beloved is a novel about collecting fragments and welding them into beautiful new wholes, about letting go of pain and guilt but also recovering what is lost and loving it into life. One of its most poignant images is the ribbon that Stamp Paid finds on the river bottom—"a red ribbon knotted around a curl of wet woolly hair, clinging still to its bit of scalp" (*Beloved*, 180). Although he knows all the horrors of 1874—the lynchings, whippings, burnings of colored schools, rapes, and lynch fires—it is this discovery which finally weakens Stamp Paid's bone marrow and makes him "dwell on Baby Suggs' wish to consider what in the world was harmless" (*Beloved*, 181).

What Morrison creates is far from harmless. She knows how painful it is to remember the horrors she presents. She has said in an interview that she expected *Beloved* to be the least read of all her books because "it is about something that the characters don't want to remember, I don't want to remember, black people don't want to remember, white people don't want to remember, I mean, it's national amnesia" (Angelo, 120). However, because *Beloved* insists on remembering, the novel is able to recover and honor the symbolic spirit of the black girl whose ribbon and piece of scalp Stamp Paid found. In so doing, it makes possible the contemplation and creation of a future in which African Americans can respect and honor themselves and their ancestors—be beloved. As Paul D says to Sethe, "Me and you, we got more yesterday than anybody. We need some kind of tomorrow" (*Beloved*, 273). What *Beloved* suggests is that tomorrow is made possible by the knowledge of yesterday, a knowledge that for contemporary African Americans can be gained from imagining what it was like to walk in the flesh of their slave ancestors.

> Auschwitz lies on the other side of life and on the other side of death. There, one lives differently, one walks differently, one dreams differently.... Only those who lived it in their flesh and their minds can possibly transform their experience into knowledge. (Wiesel, 1).

By giving its readers the inside view of slaves' lives—which bore uncanny resemblance to the Holocaust—the novel enables its African American readers to live the experience of slavery in their minds and to join in the healing primal sound of the women who come to Sethe's yard. By speaking the horror, Morrison assumes and helps to create the community that can hear it and transform it.

SUSAN COREY ON THE GROTESQUE IN *BELOVED*

In *Beloved*, one such unfamiliar reality is the interior life of Sethe, whose subjective identity has been officially discredited and denied by the dominant culture. As female and slave, she has experienced the power of whites to harm not only the physical body, but the innermost soul: she has understood that they had the power "not just [to] work, kill, or maim you, but dirty you. Dirty you so bad you couldn't like yourself any more" (251). *Beloved* gives form to such experiences of slavery that have also left indelible effects on America, a nation that continues to suffer the social and psychological consequences of this history of slavery and racism. On one level the novel explores the inner life of Sethe as she undergoes the difficult process of reformulating her identity, a process that requires her to confront not only the violence done to her, but also her own violent murder of her child. On another level, *Beloved* confronts readers with the shocking "otherness" of the slave experience, with their complicity in this tragedy, and with the consequences of attempting to set aside or forget this aspect of our national history.

The grotesque is well suited for this kind of exploration. Anti-rational by nature, the grotesque works to pierce conventional versions of reality, to undermine the status quo and everyday, agreed-upon assumptions, and to explore what we do not understand. While it is easier to describe than to define, I propose the following, drawn from Robert Doty, Geoffrey Harpham, and Mikhail Bakhtin, as a working definition: the grotesque is an aesthetic form that works through exaggeration, distortion, contradiction, disorder, and shock to disrupt a sense of normalcy and stimulate the discovery of new meaning and new connections. In its capacity to shock and offend, the grotesque exposes the depths of human vulnerability and the capacity for evil; in its capacity to evoke the realm of myth and mystery, it taps the resources of the body and the unconscious to open up new worlds of meaning and to expose the gaps in our conventional meaning systems (Doty, *Human Concern* 4; Harpham 51; Bakhtin 48). In *Beloved*, the grotesque aids Morrison in representing the complex social world of slavery and exposing the moral failure of the society which sustained and defended that institution. At the same time it opens doors for change and renewal to those who suffer the effects of slavery. Compatible with Morrison's high artistic standards, the grotesque achieves its effects through aesthetic means: visual imagery, paradox, distortion or degradation, and the clash of seemingly incompatible elements, all of which evoke a reader's heightened sense of awareness while avoiding sentimentality or moral harangue (Doty 4). (...)

Examples of the negative grotesque begin on the first page of the novel with the haunting of Sethe's home by the "baby ghost," evidence of the eruption of disorder amid the daily lives of Sethe and her family. The strange voices, lights, and violent shaking caused by this ghost have seriously disrupted the normalcy of Sethe's family life, frightening her and her daughter, Denver, and causing her sons to leave home. These opening scenes alert the reader that this story involves that border region between the mundane world and the realm of mystery or the uncanny. For Sethe the ghostly signs are concrete reminders of her guilt for the murder of her baby some eighteen years ago. The physical shaking urges her to break out of her normal routine and to confront directly this ghost of guilt from her past.

One of the most powerful grotesque images in the novel is the deforming, tree-shaped scar which Sethe bears on her back and reveals to the former slave, Paul D, soon after his arrival at 124. It is a clear example of the qualities of physical deformity, degradation, paradox, and ambiguity typically associated with the grotesque. Its decorative, viney quality recalls the style of grotesque painting discovered in the ancient Roman *grotte*, and like many grotesque images its effect is both repulsive and attractive, signifying the complexity of Sethe's relationship to her past. As the physical inscription of a brutal humiliation and beating by the slave master, Schoolteacher, the scar recalls the horror of that historical past. In order to support his theory of racial inferiority, Schoolteacher had ordered his nephews to "take [Sethe's] milk" as part of an experiment to demonstrate the "animal" characteristics of blacks. Sethe was not only required to submit to this degradation, but also to participate by making the ink with which Schoolteacher recorded the results of his experiments. This scene shocks the reader with unspeakable horror and serves as a prime example of slavery's destructive effects on the imagination and the inner life. As Sethe reflects, the whites could "dirty you so bad you forgot who you were and couldn't think it up" (251). The deadened scar tissue on Sethe's back is emblematic of her repressed feelings related to this experience. The taking of her milk has affected her more profoundly than the physical beating that followed. As she recalls, "The picture of the men coming to nurse her was as lifeless as the nerves in her back where the skin buckled like a washboard" (6). The scar, then, becomes a bodily sign of Sethe's estrangement from her imagination and her inner life. Like the deadened nerves that alienate her from her bodily sensations, the "lifeless" picture represents the blocked memory and emotions that separate her from a full, subjective identity. As an element of the grotesque, the scar also functions as a sign of degradation, which Bakhtin explains as the process of bringing an elevated ideal or quality down to earth, to the physical level (20–22). In this respect, the scar and its link to the "experiment" on Sethe degrades both the ideology of slavery and the "Christian" society that upheld it by exposing the brutal consequences of those theories on the interior as well as the exterior lives of its victims.

However, Morrison maintains a dialectical tension in her use of this image—it is not merely negative. In its resemblance to a tree, the scar recalls the natural beauty and the qualities of comfort and renewal that Sethe associates with her former home. Unable to see the scar herself, Sethe remembers that Amy, the white girl who delivered her baby, described it as a blossoming tree—"'Your back got a whole tree on it. In bloom'" (79)—and she repeats Amy's words to Paul D: "'a chokecherry tree. Trunk, branches, and even leaves'" (79). In Sethe's mind, the tree might even be bearing fruit: "'Could have cherries too now for all I know,'" she tells Paul D (16). In this respect, the scar acts as the positive grotesque, suggesting the possibilities of renewal through the natural cyclical processes of the body, a prominent theme for Bakhtin, for whom the grotesque affirms the human con-nection to "the material and bodily roots of the world" (19).

Paul D also experiences the ambiguous effects of the scar. He sees it first as a wrought iron sculpture filled with unexpressed emotion, "like the decorative work of an ironsmith too passionate for display" (17). When he touches the tree-like scar with his cheek, he contacts Sethe's deep sadness: he feels "her sorrow, the roots of it; its wide trunk and intricate branches" (17). Later, however, it appears to be simply "a revolting clump of scars," nothing like a tree, since trees were "inviting; things you could trust and be near; talk to if you wanted to" (21).

These contradictory connotations of the scar suggest the ambiguity of Sethe's relationship to the landscapes of her past, a relationship reinforced by her memory of the beautiful sycamore trees of Sweet Home, treasured despite their painful association with the hangings of her fellow slaves: "Although there was not a leaf on that farm that did not make her want to scream, it rolled itself out before her in shameless beauty.... Boys hanging from the most beautiful sycamores in the world. It shamed her—remembering the wonderful soughing trees rather than the boys" (6). Through the imagery of trees, an experience of horror and degradation is linked to a contrasting picture of beauty, comfort, and the ongoing life of the natural world. This clash of incompatible elements is a salient feature of the grotesque, contributing to its interpretive energy by stimulating readers to discover new connections and new meaning (Harpham 187).

In its negative mode, then, the scar is an emblem of Sethe's suffering, degradation, and fear which has marked her psychically as well as physically. As such, it links her to a number of other characters who bear grotesque deformities, bodily signs of their inner suffering: Baby Suggs, who had injured her hip as a slave and walked with a limp; Sethe's mother, Ma'am, who bore the burned mark of a cross on her skin; Nan, Sethe's wet nurse, who was missing half of one arm; Ella, marked with "scars from the bell ... thick as a rope around her waist" (258); and Paul D, who carried the mark of the iron collar on his neck, "three wands like attentive baby rattlers curving two feet into the air" (2–73; see Ledbetter 42–45). These physical deformities, all marks of the grotesque, serve to heighten the reader's consciousness of the monstrous character of slavery written on the bodies of its victims. In its positive or "comic" mode, however, the scar signifies the renewing processes of life: in this case, the mystery and wonder of Sethe's survival and renewed strength as she gives birth to Denver and journeys toward Baby Suggs and freedom in Ohio, a journey with mythic overtones recalling the birth of Moses and the Israelites' journey out of Egypt.

Throughout the novel, Morrison sustains a dialectical tension between these two modes of the grotesque, not allowing her fiction to rest in either one. The moments of renewal and hope tend to dissolve into scenes of fear and alienation. Even Sethe's hopeful journey has its negative side, leading ultimately to the moment of madness when she murders her baby—a grotesque event in its shocking violence, and one that renders Sethe a grotesque figure in the eyes of her community. In the various accounts of this event, Morrison employs the paradoxical features of the grotesque to present a complex vision of Sethe's community. Like Bakhtin and his model, Rabelais, she celebrates the potential of the community to provide resources for renewal and hope and to sustain traditional folk values. However, Morrison is critical of the community's failure to love and forgive. She portrays the community's failure to grasp the broader context of Sethe's act or to empathize with her conviction that death would be preferable to life under slavery. Rather than looking within, the community projects its fears onto Sethe, casting her as a grotesque figure who has transgressed all bounds of normalcy and, together with her family, must be strictly avoided. This critical perspective on the community is an example of an important quality of the grotesque in African-American literature: "the simultaneous presence of a total involvement in the black experience and its critical appraisal from an extreme emotional distance" (Gysin 89–90). The grotesque always insists on the mixed nature of human existence.

The most obviously grotesque character in the novel and the one most responsible for introducing dissonance and shock into the lives of the protagonists is Beloved. As the physical embodiment of Sethe's murdered daughter, as well as those thousands who died during the middle passage, Beloved resembles one of the African river goddesses who easily crosses boundaries between the living and the dead (see Cliff). She represents the eruption of the uncanny, the anti-rational, or the mythic into the realm of normal existence, an event that may unlock previously locked emotions and open the mind to a wider experience of life. According to traditional African cosmology, Beloved could also be a potentially dangerous spirit because of her unnatural death. Peter Paris writes that in African cosmology those who die an unnatural death cannot be ancestors; hence a spirit who suffers an unnatural death is capricious and "not easily pacified" since it has lost its family and community moorings (52–53).

Like other grotesques, Beloved is a contradictory figure—positive and negative, attractive and repulsive. Both beautiful and freakish, she is abnormally strong with expressionless eyes, capable of changing shape and character or of becoming invisible. As a positive or comic grotesque, Beloved functions in the realm of fantasy and interior space where she promotes healing and growth for Sethe and Paul D, both of whom have closed off their emotional lives following their traumatic past experiences. Their contact with Beloved raises questions they have avoided and sets in motion the recovery of repressed memories, a connection that is painful but crucial for the process of rebuilding self identity. Beloved's questions direct Sethe to memories of her past, so painful that it was previously "unspeakable" (58); they lead Paul D to the "ocean-deep place he had once belonged to" (264), a level of reality beyond language. Yet Beloved also contributes to the dialectical tension between the positive and negative grotesque. She is dangerous in her exaggerated neediness, her desire to possess Sethe completely and to take her to "the other side." Her demands magnify Sethe's mother-guilt and encourage her obsessive effort to make amends for the murder to the point of nearly giving up her life, becoming death-focused and mired in the past.

Beloved first appears in fleshly form in the context of a carnival, an event closely associated with the positive grotesque. In Bakhtin's view, the medieval spirit of carnival embodies the basic impulse for the grotesque: it frees the world from fear and offers temporary liberation from the established hierarchies of class and rank (10, 19). Beloved appears immediately after Paul D, Sethe, and her daughter Denver return from such a carnival. Performed for an all-black audience on "Colored Thursday," the carnival has temporarily upset the social order. The audience has laughed at the grotesque characters, temporarily dethroning the ideal of white supremacy: "seeing white people loose: doing magic, clowning, without heads or with two heads, twenty feet tall or two feet tall" (47–48). Despite having to endure a few insults themselves, the black community has enjoyed laughing at "the spectacle of white folks making a spectacle of themselves" (48). In Bakhtin's model, laughter is a means of overcoming fear and celebrating a common humanity (11, 47). In the same way, the carnival laughter has allowed the black community to erase temporarily any fear of white folks' "otherness" and to view them from a new perspective. It has even altered some intra-community attitudes: Denver notices that after eighteen years of shunning, some women have dared to smile at Sethe (48). For Bakhtin, the carnival prepares the way for change by freeing the imagination to play with an alternative world view (49). In this sense it is a fitting prelude to the arrival of Beloved, who disrupts the lives of Sethe and her family and opens them to the possibility of change and renewal.

Images of the open body are further signs of Beloved's affinity with the positive grotesque. Immediately after Beloved arrives, Sethe experiences strong, physical symptoms of release—an uncontrollable urge to urinate, followed by a rush of water so strange and overwhelming that she feels like a carnival freak. Beloved herself consumes large quantities of water, followed by episodes of incontinence during her four days of deep sleep (51, 54). These images of bodily release are examples of what Bakhtin calls the grotesque body—the open body of becoming that affirms connections with the material and bodily roots of the world. In his analysis, images of eating and drinking or of open bodily orifices suggest openness to the world and the ongoing processes of life (26–27, 281). Yet

Beloved has an equal affinity with the negative grotesque or the uncanny. She is a fascinating playmate for Denver until, in a game of hide-and-seek, Denver is terrified by Beloved's ability to magically appear and disappear (123). For Sethe and Paul D, Beloved serves as a catalyst to awaken their emotions and memories, but she also arouses their fears. Her dual aspects are continually apparent.

Paul D discerns an uncanny quality about Beloved from the outset as she sets out to take his place beside Sethe. Soon after her arrival, he finds himself being mysteriously moved out of Sethe's house, even as he had earlier evicted the "baby ghost." In the darkness of the cold house, where he has come to spend his nights, Beloved mysteriously appears and subjects him to a grotesque seduction, insisting that he touch her "inside part" and call her name (117). He resists her overtures, just as he resists confronting the painful memories of his last days at Sweet Home—the sight of his closest companions hung, sold, or reduced to idiocy, and the brutalizing experiences on the chain gang. Feeling ashamed and guilty over these encounters with Beloved, Paul D experiences physical signs of her uncanny effect—"a shudder" and "a bone cold spasm" (235)—when Stamp Paid mentions her name.

Nevertheless, these sexual encounters are important for Paul D's recovery of self. The arousal of his bodily responses is accompanied by an awakening of his emotion and memories: the lid of the "tobacco tin" protecting his heart gives way, leaving him vulnerable to the repressed emotions from his past—his feelings of guilt at his failure to join Sixo, who had laughed in the face of fear; and his shame at being harnessed with a bit, so that even Brother, the rooster, seemed to laugh at him. Although confronting these memories is exceedingly painful, Paul D later admits his gratefulness to Beloved for escorting him toward that "ocean-deep" place (264). Through his contact with her, Paul D has begun to reconnect to his body, his emotions, and his unconscious memories.

The effect of Beloved on Sethe is more complex, although similarly ambiguous. Beloved's questions and her demand for stories stimulate Sethe's memories of her childhood and her own mother, whom she barely knew. In telling these stories, Sethe experiences an awakening of pain and anger as she recalls the mother who was not allowed time to nurse her, the mother who was hanged for some unknown offense. Yet the stories also evoke positive memories—events or images that suggest hope for renewed ties with the community or with the lost or repressed part of the self.

Works by Toni Morrison

The Bluest Eye, 1970.

Sula, 1974.

The Black Book, 1974 (conceived and edited).

Song of Solomon, 1977.

Tar Baby, 1981.

New Orleans (musical), 1983.

Dreaming Emmett (play), 1986.

Beloved, 1987.

Jazz, 1992.

Race-ing Justice, En-Gendering Power, 1992 (edited and
 contributed).

Playing in the Dark: Whiteness and the Literary Imagination,
 1992.

Honey and Rue (song cycle), 1993.

*Birth of a Nation'hood: Gaze, Script, and Spectacle in the O.J.
 Simpson Case* (co-edited with Claudia Brodsky Lacour),
 1997.

Paradise, 1998.

Annotated Bibliography

Askeland, Lori. "Remodeling the Model Home in *Uncle Tom's Cabin* and *Beloved*," *American Literature* 64, no. 4 (January 1992): 785–805.

Askeland notes similarities in *Uncle Tom's Cabin* and *Beloved*, focusing on settings, while also pointing out how Morrison's fiction revises and reimagines Stowe's.

Birat, Kathie. "Stories to Pass On: Closure and Community in Toni Morrison's *Beloved*," *The Insular Dream: Obsession and Resistance*. Kristiaan Versluys, ed. Amsterdam: VU University Press, 1995. pp. 324–334.

Birat explains how the novel's narrative strategies reflects how Morrison views slavery as a disruption of all the normal processes of human experiences. As the narrative uses postmodern techniques, reconstructing while deconstructing, *Beloved* rewrites the history of slavery.

Bjork, Patrick Bryce. "Beloved: The Paradox of a Past and Present Self and Place," *The Novels Of Toni Morrison: The Search for Self and Place Within the Community*. New York: Peter Lang, 1992.

Bjork examines the role of community in *Beloved*, arguing that identity and place are found not in claiming individuality but within community. Bjork focuses on the character of Beloved as a communal memory.

Davis, Kimberly Chabot. "'Postmodern Blackness'": Toni Morrison's *Beloved* and the End of History," *Twentieth Century Literature* 44, no. 2 (Summer 1998): 242–260.

This essay examines how the novel exhibits a postmodern skepticism of sweeping historical narratives, while also retaining an African American and modernist political commitment to the crucial importance of cultural memory.

Furman, Jan. *Toni Morrison's Fiction*. Columbia, SC: University of South Carolina Press, 1996.

This book provides a basic introduction to Morrison's work. The chapter on *Beloved* examines how Morrison delineates Sethe as a strong woman and portrays the lives of slaves in a way that had not been done before.

Harris, Trudier. *Fiction and Folklore: The Novels of Toni Morrison*. Knoxville: University of Tennessee Press, 1991.

Harris examines the use of Beloved as a shapeshifter, the structure and power of storytelling, and the myth of Sweet Home.

Henderson, Mae. G. "Toni Morrison's *Beloved*: Re-Membering the Body as Historical Text," *Comparative American Identities: Race, Sex, and Nationality in the Modern Text*. Hortense J. Spillers, ed. New York: Routledge, 1991. pp. 62–86.

Henderson examines the novel in the context of contemporary historical theory on discourse and narrative and offers a reading that links historiography and psychoanalysis.

Holden-Kirwan, Jennifer L. "Looking into the Self That Is No Self: An Examination of Subjectivity in *Beloved*," *African American Review* 32, no. 3 (Fall 1998): 415–426.

Holden-Kirwan explores the question of Beloved's identity and how her identity affects her own subjectivity, as well as that of Denver and Sethe.

Keizer, Arlene R. "*Beloved*: Ideologies in Conflict, Improvised Subjects," *African American Review* 33, no. 1 (Spring 1999): 105–123.

Keizer examines the way *Beloved* attempts to define a position for the black subject between essentialism and postmodern fragmentation.

Kolmerten, Carol A., Stephen M. Ross and Judith Bryant Wittenberg, eds. *Unflinching Gaze: Morrison and Faulkner Re-envisioned*. Jackson: University of Mississippi, 1997.

A collection of critical essays that explore the intertextual relationship between the fiction of William Faulkner and that of Toni Morrison.

Mandel, Naomi. "'I Made the Ink': Identity, Complicity, 60 Million, and More." *Modern Fiction Studies* 48, no. 3 (Fall 2002): 581–613.

Mandel questions whether *Beloved* articulates the horrors of slavery, or retreats "into a privileged space of silence."

Mobley, Marilyn Sanders. "A Different Remembering: Memory, History, and Meaning in Beloved," *Modern Critical Views: Toni Morrison.* Harold Bloom, ed. New York: Chelsea House, 1990). pp. 189–199.

Mobley examines the intertextual relationship between *Beloved* and the slave narratives and shows how Morrison uses the trope of memory to revise the genre of the slave narrative. Morrison uses memory to explore interior life and to represent dimensions of slave life that classic slave narratives omitted.

Ochoa, Peggy. "Morrison's *Beloved*: Allegorically Othering 'White' Christianity," *MELUS* 24, no. 2 (Summer 1999): 107–123.

Ochoa examines the use of Biblical allegory in *Beloved.*

Otten, Terry. *The Crime of Innocence in the Fiction of the Toni Morrison.* Columbia: University of Missouri Press, 1991.

The chapter on *Beloved* focuses on how the narrative depicts the complex relationship between good and evil and documents the historical plight of blacks in America.

Page, Philip. "Anything Dead Coming Back to Life Hurts: Circularity in *Beloved*," *Dangerous Freedom.* Jackson, Miss.: University Press of Mississippi, 1995. pp. 133–158.

Page addresses themes of fusion and fragmentation in *Beloved*, examining how the narrative structure provides insight into the novel's content, form, and context.

Pérez-Torres, Rafael. "Between Presence and Absence: Beloved, Postmodernism, and Blackness," *Toni Morrison's Beloved: A Casebook*. William L. Andrews and Nellie Y. McKay, eds. New York: Oxford University Press, 1999.

The article examines the paradox in trying to articulate black identity in a language in which blackness is a figure of absence.

Pesch, Josef. "*Beloved*: Toni Morrison's Post-Apocalyptic Novel," *Canadian Review of Contemporary Literature* 20, no. 3–4 (September–December 1993): 395–408.

Pesch examines *Beloved* as a post-apocalyptic narrative, which means the story focuses on past instead of future.

Phelan, James. "Sethe's Choice: *Beloved* and the Ethics of Reading," *Mapping the Ethical Turn: A Reader in Ethics, Culture, and Literary Theory*. Todd F. Davis and Kenneth Womack, eds. Charlottesville, VA: University Press of Virginia, 2001. pp. 93–109.

Phelan focuses on Sethe's murdering her baby and the ethical questions it raises.

Rody, Caroline. "Toni Morrison's *Beloved*: History, 'Rememory,' and a 'Clamor for a Kiss,'" *American Literary History* 7, no. 1 (Spring 1995): 92–119.

Rody focuses on *Beloved*'s historical content.

Rushdy, Ashrafi. "Daughters Signifyin(g) History: The Example of Toni Morrison's *Beloved*," *American Literature* 64, no. 3 (September 1992): 567–597.

Rushdy looks at Morrison's revisionist return to history and the concept of memory and argues that Beloved gives the dead a voice.

Sale, Roger. "Toni Morrison's Beloved." *Massachusetts Review* 29, no. 1 (Spring 1988): 71–86.

Sale examines the structure of *Beloved* as story, elegy, and "rememory."

Smith, Valerie. "'Circling the Subject': History and Narrative in *Beloved*," *Toni Morrison: Critical Perspectives Past and Present*. Henry Louis Gates, Jr. and K.A. Appiah, eds. New York: Amistad, 1993: 342–355.

Smith situates *Beloved* within a larger investigation of representation and experience, discourse and slavery. *Beloved* shows the body in pain and narrates the impossibility of speaking the unspeakable.

Contributors

Harold Bloom is Sterling Professor of the Humanities at Yale University and Henry W. and Albert A. Berg Professor of English at the New York University Graduate School. He is the author of over 20 books, including *Shelley's Mythmaking* (1959), *The Visionary Company* (1961), *Blake's Apocalypse* (1963), *Yeats* (1970), *A Map of Misreading* (1975), *Kabbalah and Criticism* (1975), *Agon: Toward a Theory of Revisionism* (1982), *The American Religion* (1992), *The Western Canon* (1994), and *Omens of Millennium: The Gnosis of Angels, Dreams, and Resurrection* (1996). *The Anxiety of Influence* (1973) sets forth Professor Bloom's provocative theory of the literary relationships between the great writers and their predecessors. His most recent books include *Shakespeare: The Invention of the Human* (1998), a 1998 National Book Award finalist, *How to Read and Why* (2000), *Genius: A Mosaic of One Hundred Exemplary Creative Minds* (2002), and *Hamlet: Poem Unlimited* (2003). In 1999, Professor Bloom received the prestigious American Academy of Arts and Letters Gold Medal for Criticism, and in 2002 he received the Catalonia International Prize.

Karla F. C. Holloway is Dean of the Humanities and Social Sciences at Duke University, where she holds the William R. Kenan Professorship of English and African American Studies. She is the author of five books, including *Passed On: African American Mourning Stories; Codes of Conduct: Race, Ethics and the Color of Our Character*; and *Moorings and Metaphors: Figures of Culture and Gender in Black Women's Literature*.

Bernard W. Bell is Professor of English at Pennsylvania State University. His most recent book is *Clarence Major and His Art* (2000). His other books include *Call and Response: The African American Literary Tradition*, *Contemporary Literature in the African Diaspora*, and *The Afro-American Novel and Its Tradition*.

Linda Krumholz teaches contemporary American literature at Denison University with an emphasis on African American, Native American, and ethnic literatures of the United States. Her publications on Toni Morrison and Leslie Marmon Silko have appeared in the *African American Review*, *Ariel*, and *Modern Fiction Studies*.

Trudier Harris is Professor of English at the University of North Carolina, Chapel Hill. Her many books include *Fiction and Folklore: The Novels of Toni Morrison* and *Exorcising Blackness: Historical and Literary Lynching and Burning Rituals*.

Pamela E. Barnett is Assistant Professor of English at the University of South Carolina, is the author of articles in *Women's Studies* and *Signs*.

Nancy Jesser teaches in the Division of Comparative Studies at The Ohio State University.

J. Brooks Bouson is Associate Professor of English at Loyola University in Chicago. She is the author of *The Empathetic Reader: A Study of the Narcissistic Character and the Drama of the Self* and *Brutal Choreographies: Oppositional Strategies and Narrative Design in the Novels of Margaret Atwood*.

Susan Bowers is Associate Professor of English and Director of Women's Studies at Susquehanna University.

Susan Corey has published essays on Toni Morrison and has co-edited two collections of American diaries and letters: *The American Journey: U.S. History in Letters and Diaries*, volumes I and II, and *Writing Women's Lives: American Women's History in Letters and Diaries*.

Acknowledgments

Holloway, Karla F. C. *"Beloved*: A Spiritual." From *Callaloo* 13, no. 3 (Summer 1990): 516–525. © 1990 by Charles H. Rowell. Reprinted with the permission of The Johns Hopkins University Press.

"Beloved: A Womanist Neo-Slave Narrative; or Multivocal Remembrances of Things Past," by Bernard W. Bell. From *African American Review* 26, no. 1 (Spring 1992): 7–15. © 1992 by Bernard W. Bell. Reprinted by permission.

"The Ghosts of Slavery: Historical Recovery in Toni Morrison's *Beloved*," by Linda Krumholz. From *African American Review* 26, no. 3 (Autumn 1992): 395–408. © 1992 by Linda Krumholz. Reprinted by permission.

"Escaping Slavery but Not Its Images," by Trudier Harris. From *Toni Morrison: Critical Perspectives Past and Present.* Henry Louis Gates, Jr. and K.A. Appiah, eds. New York: Amistad Press, 1993. pp. 330–341. © 1993 by Henry Louis Gates, Jr. and K.A. Appiah. Reprinted by permission.

"Figurations of Rape and the Supernatural in *Beloved*," by Pamela E Barnett. From *PMLA* 112, no. 3 (May 1997): 418–427. © 1997 by The Modern Language Association of America. Reprinted by permission.

"Violence, Home, and Community in Toni Morrison's *Beloved*," by Nancy Jesser. From *African American Review* 33, no. 2 (Summer 1999): 325–345. © 1999 by Nancy Jesser. Reprinted by permission.

"'Whites Might Dirty Her All Right, but Not Her Best Thing': The Dirtied and Traumatized Self of Slavery in *Beloved*." Reprinted by permission from *Quiet As It's Kept:*

Index